MW00634603

Letting Go

How One Entrepreneur Energized Her Business, Empowered the Next Generation, and Embraced a Bold New Vision

For Anne — looking forward to working together + getting to know you.
Warmly,
Susan Sokol Blosser

susan sokol blosser

LETTING GO: How One Entrepreneur Energized Her Business, Empowered the Next Generation, and Embraced a Bold New Vision

ISBN #978-0-9908888-0-2

Cover photo © Doreen L. Wynja, www.eyeofthelady.com.
Taken outside the Sokol Blosser Winery Tasting Room.

Interior photos courtesy of the author unless otherwise noted.

Cover and interior design: Bridget Backus McBride,
www.spotteddogcreative.com

Printed in the USA.
Your Town Press, Salem, Oregon,
www.yourtownpress.com

dedication

To Heidi, Ingrid, and Lauren,
who played important roles in this period of my life.

Thank you, my friends,
for your caring and your wisdom.

table of contents

Acknowledgements

Special friends and family took time to read my manuscript in its formative stages, giving me their perspective and constructive feedback. Susan Barnes Whyte, Lauren McCall, Brian Doyle all took time to read and give me feedback. Heidi Yorkshire, my tough love friend, stayed with me through multiple revisions. My brother, Ronald Sokol, gave me the benefit of his fierce intellect, fulfilling his lifelong role as my teacher. Kim Stafford, although exceptionally busy with his own book debut, took time to buoy me at a particularly low point, giving me renewed hope and energy. Debra Gwartney helped me ask the right questions. Lee Montgomery provided invaluable editorial assistance. Enormous thanks to my family – Bill, Nik, Alex, Alison – who made suggestions and let me tell their stories as part of mine. And to Russ, my friend, lover, and editor I couldn't live without. I am deeply grateful to all.

1

The Baton

A hush settled over the room as I stood up and clinked two wine glasses together. The clear ring of two crystal surfaces reverberating against each other had the desired effect. Twenty-five Sokol Blosser Winery employees and family members stopped their chatter and looked up from their desserts. January 2nd, 2008, our first day back at work in the New Year. I hated to interrupt the conviviality of a special catered lunch, but I needed to complete my mission. A little over three years before, I initiated the process of turning over control of the family business, a vineyard and winery, to my children. Today would be my last day as President; two of my children would take over as Co-presidents.

At the time of my decision, it sounded straightforward; give the kids more experience and hand over the reins. Instead, I climbed onto an emotional roller coaster, uprooting issues at the core of my being. More complicated and difficult than anticipated, I told myself I had to set an example for my children, who someday would pass what they had built on to their children. Like all of us, they too would have to face letting go of their power.

A month earlier, I had looked at the calendar and realized that the practice year was almost over. What my son and daughter, Alex and Alison, had been referring to as "flipping the switch" was only a few weeks away. The gracious thing to do would be to organize a luncheon for the staff. Hosting the official ceremony and giving my blessing would be my last presidential act.

I sent personal invitations to all the people I thought should attend. Then I started to worry. I alternated between feeling savvy, even masterful, and then suddenly wanting to curl up in the fetal position in the dark quiet of my clothes closet. But this was no time to crumble. Determined to finish what I had started, I called myself a Gloomy Kerplopus and tried to laugh.

Before speaking, I looked across the room, smiling at the upturned familiar faces of all the people I had hired and worked with every day. I was at one end of the informal head table, along with the Sokol Blosser family. On my left, tall, athletic, charismatic Alex sat next to his delicately featured, more serious younger sister, Alison, whose calm demeanor concealed her fierce drive and determination. Both children were undoubtedly anxious for the ceremony to begin; they had been preparing for this moment since 2004.

On the other side of Alex and Alison, Bill Blosser, my former husband, the dreamer who first suggested in 1970 that he and I, a young married couple, start a vineyard, looked up from his dessert. Leaning slightly forward to see me, his eyes had a distant expression, like he wasn't with us. I assumed it reflected his detachment, having been only peripherally involved with the winery for the seventeen years since I had been at the helm. It had been Bill's early vision and passion that had carried us for the first two decades. But his flame slowly burned out as the reality of Oregon winemaking proved harder than anticipated. When that happened and Bill stepped down, I took over as president. Now, years later, with his children taking over what he had started, I hoped the time could be right for his passion to return.

I stole a quick glance at Russ Rosner, our winemaker since 1998, my domestic partner since 1999, and my husband since 2007. Russ sat with his cellar crew. I caught his eye and knew that behind his stern, impassive veneer, lay a fierce caring, wishing me strength. With my notes in front of me, in case my mind went blank, I began. "Thank you for being here today to celebrate this very special occasion." I was surprised at how easily that came out and how suddenly sanguine I felt. With a surge of energy, I continued. There were things I wanted to say about Sokol Blosser's new co-presidents.

Although they might be considered too young to take over the presidency of a multi-million dollar business, Alex, thirty-four, and Alison, twenty-eight, had been training for this all their lives. At the age of five, Alison crawled inside the wine press to help her father clean it. I had watched her walk down from our house to the winery, traipsing through the vineyard in the early evening, her little hand holding tightly to her father's. Bill in his jeans, cotton shirt, and boots; Alison in pink shorts, T-shirt and tennis shoes, moving in and out of the shadows cast by the sun setting over the hillside. The easiest way to clean the press was to get inside and hose it down. Adults were too large and could only lean in and aim the hose. When Bill had asked if she wanted to climb inside the press and help, Alison eagerly agreed. Joyful at being able to do something none of the adults could do, she beamed with pride when she returned home, heedless of being soaked to the skin. That little girl had become the bright young woman sitting next to me, ready to take on the world.

I also remembered ten-year-old Alex sitting at a small table at the entrance to our tasting room, welcoming guests and collecting entrance fees at our Wine Country Thanksgiving Open House. We had coached him on what to say but our sociable son scripted his own patter. "Welcome to Sokol Blosser," he said, his dimples lighting up his face as he smiled. "Would you like to buy a ticket to taste our wines?" Who could resist? Watching from behind the bar where I was serving wine, I could see our guests melt at his earnestness. He stuck it out and, after the long three-day weekend, had welcomed enough guests to lose his voice. He also earned enough money to buy the Space Lego set he'd coveted in the Lego catalog. Alex never shied from hard work. He accumulated an impressive amount of Lego, which he still plays, now with his twin sons.

This day held so much meaning for me. I was a different person from the one who took over in 1991. Older, more confident, with accomplishment under my belt, I felt the poignancy of giving up the position that had shaped me and defined my persona. Turning the presidency over to Alex and Alison had further significance. It meant we had become a family business, enduring long enough to enter the second generation.

Survival was never assured and often in doubt. When people asked how the business was going, I usually answered, "We're still here." I smiled as I said it, but I wasn't being flippant. Staying afloat for the first thirty years was a constant challenge. We were often dangerously close to the edge. In 1990, just before I became president, the winery was deeply in debt; inflation had raised the interest on our loan to twenty-three percent. That gobbled up our meager cash flow, already sparse with the economic slump. "We're still here," was a statement of survival.

Outside, the rain pelted the branches of the bare bigleaf maples, but the somber weather couldn't dampen our spirits. Today was about celebration, a landmark day for the winery and for Alex and Alison. I had been aware of Alex glancing sideways at me during lunch, and of Alison smoothing invisible wrinkles in the cloth napkin in her lap. I wondered if they had as many butterflies as I did seventeen years ago.

After my introduction, Bill stood up to speak. He was as slim and carefully dressed as he'd been when we first met as college students at Stanford. I had a sudden image of him back then, fresh from his year in France, tall, dark, and sexy, with his prized French beret perfectly tilted on his head. His hair was now silver and his face more worn, but he still lit up when he smiled. His eyes took on warmth when he talked about his children, about how hard they had worked to help in the vineyard and the winery, and how appropriate this new opportunity would be for them and the business.

Then it was Alison's turn. Her quiet voice quavered as she started, thanking Bill and me for the privilege and important charge they had been given. Normally jovial, Alex was unexpectedly solemn, his voice trembling part way through. I was gratified to see they both clearly felt the weight of their new roles.

Several of the longtime winery staff also stood to make toasts, including Russ who, after some pleasantries, ended with a warning to the new presidents "not to screw it up." I knew he was deadly serious but he said it playfully and everyone laughed. The energy in the room felt friendly, warm, and hopeful. In answer to my concern whether Alex's five-year-old twins could sit still for the ceremony, Avery and Nikolas were quiet and attentive. Having the third generation present reinforced the family feeling.

Years before, one of our employees with a good sense of humor had made Bill a wooden club with a little brass plaque inscribed "Administrative Tool." It resembled a medieval mace and had been intended as a joke, but we treated it like a royal scepter, with a place of honor in my office. I had it on the table next to me. "This is for you now," I said, as I put the Administrative Tool ceremoniously into Alex and Alison's hands. With this symbolic gift, I formally inaugurated the second generation's control. It felt like such a momentous occasion I half expected church bells to ring or someone to shout "The Queen is dead, Long Live the Queen!" My reign was over. January 2, 1991 to January 2, 2008, seventeen years to the day since I became president. A small quiver of excitement surged through me. We had successfully executed what, to the entire world, appeared a seamless transition.

As the party broke up and everyone went back to work, I couldn't stop smiling. The press release had gone out in an email that morning. I spent the afternoon in my office answering notes from media friends who wished me well. I expected to be depressed, but the smile that emerged when I passed the baton presaged a new emotion which surged through me: liberation. This delicious sensation made me realize how much I'd held back, directing all my emotional energy towards the winery. Now, as if moving the tuner to clear the channel, the static that had filled my brain for the past thirty-eight years was gone. New sounds were coming in. My mind was free to soar. I couldn't believe what had just happened. I had let go.

2

Birth — Vineyard, Family, Industry

Bill and I didn't intend to start a family business. We weren't thinking that far ahead. The idea surfaced unexpectedly in Amish country, the summer of 1970. We were heading back to Oregon in our Volkswagen camper after two years in graduate school at the University of North Carolina at Chapel Hill. Bill was bringing his newly conferred Masters Degree of City and Regional Planning. I, newly pregnant, was carrying our first child. We had stopped in southeastern Pennsylvania to browse at a flea market when Bill turned to me.

"Know what I'd like to do? I'd like to buy some land and plant a vineyard." He gave me an odd smile, suggesting, questioning, imploring at the same time. The antique clock in my hands lost its interest as I let his comment sink in. Had anyone else heard this wild statement? I looked around; no one was paying attention to us. The dust on the fairgrounds swirled past my legs, landing on the vendors' tables laden with old junk, or potential treasures, depending on one's perspective. I turned back to my inquiring husband, who appeared fascinated by a pair of antique tongs. He looked up with a sly smile. "Wouldn't it be great to have a vineyard and grow wine grapes? Why not?"

I didn't know how to respond. Starting a vineyard would not have been my choice. This was a wild, impractical idea. We knew nothing about farming or growing grapes. Neither of us had any experience making wine, nor any business or financial training. Why would we want to start an agricultural business? I wanted to be a supportive wife, a good life partner, so I didn't say what I thought. Instead, I let that casual conversation, which seemed to come from nowhere, determine our path. Our vineyard was born in that flea market, and it happened fast. Unhindered by knowledge or experience, armed only with Bill's passion and my desire to support him, we pursued the idea until we made it happen. We rented a house in Portland when we arrived in August and spent weekends driving the countryside looking for property. We didn't quite know what to look for, knowing only that we needed land that would escape late spring frosts. Hillside orchards would work since fruit trees bloomed in the spring. Grapes didn't need the rich bottom land soil, but they could thrive in frost-free pockets on south and east facing hillsides.

In mid-December 1970, we bought our first piece of land destined to be Sokol Blosser Vineyard, an eighteen acre abandoned prune orchard. Within two weeks, we also had our first child, Nik. We were both twenty-six years old, and I thought of it as each of us giving birth. In retrospect, it strikes me as odd that I saw it as his and hers, rather than thinking of us together birthing two babies. The gestations were almost simultaneous, the vineyard's being three months shorter from idea to reality.

The spring of 1971, when Nik was five months old, we loaded up our 1954 Chevy pickup with our worldly goods, our infant son and two cats, and moved the thirty-five miles from Portland to a rural community called Dayton, where we rented a farm house near our property. It was the fifth house we had lived in during our five years of marriage. This time we were going to put down roots. Literally.

Bill rooted the cuttings we had bought in California in the large front yard of our rented home the first summer, while we cleared the land. Those rootings constituted our first vineyard planting the following April, the earliest that spring we could work the ground and lay out the rows. Bill's parents, aunt and uncle, sister and cousins came to help. Under the gray skies of an Oregon spring, with the threat of the clouds opening up at any moment, we spent the day putting our first vines in the ground. Bill had drilled the planting holes the day before, so all we had to do was walk to the hole, kneel down to put the little rooting in the soil close to the wooden peg, mound up dirt around it, straighten up, walk six feet to the next marker and repeat the process. By the end of the day, we had sore backs and three acres of little sticks with swollen buds poking up out of the dirt in long rows.

As the weather warmed, the little sticks sent out green shoots. Having no irrigation didn't matter as there was enough Oregon spring rain. We tried to visit our vines often, but sometimes a week would go by without a visit. Our vineyard was taking shape, but the vines weren't the only thing growing.

About a month after planting, when Bill got home from his job in Portland, we bundled up baby Nik and drove our pickup the two miles up the hill to our new vineyard. When we got out of the truck to admire our new vines, they were nowhere to be seen. Close to panic, we looked at each other with sudden understanding. We knew where the rows of vines should be, but all we could see was a mat of slender lacy greens covered with tiny purple flowers. Our little vines had disappeared under the native vetch. It had happened fast, as soon as the weather had warmed the wet, fertile soil. Between Bill's job and my caring for our baby, we had missed the narrow window to hoe the weeds before they overran the vines. The labor it took to rescue the baby vines from beneath the vetch and other native grasses drove home an important farming lesson: farming practices needed to be done when nature dictated, not when we found it convenient.

We started and ended the decade of the 1970s with the birth of a child. As that decade wound down, Bill and I had a vineyard, three children (Nik in 1970, Alex in 1974, and Alison in 1979), and a fledgling winery. Our university degrees hadn't provided much practical guidance. We learned to farm by trial and error, along with the handful of other young urban professionals, the Letts, Eraths, Courys, Campbells, Ponzis, Adelsheims, and Fuquas, who had the same harebrained idea we did.

For years, I tried to answer the inevitable, obvious question of how Bill and I decided, with no experience, to start a vineyard in a state that had no wine industry, and grow a grape that had never done well in the United States. I didn't really understand it myself and usually ended up joking that we had more guts than brains, or that it was the kind of thing you do when you're young and think you can do anything. Those feeble explanations never felt right. We were Stanford graduates; we researched Oregon's potential for vineyards; we were prepared to risk everything for our experiment. Something more than a youthful lark propelled us forward.

With hindsight, I have been able to place us in the social context of the late 1960s and early 1970s. History will record it as a decade of violent political strife, with civil rights riots, assassinations, and Vietnam War protests, all leading to significant social change. But less headline-grabbing arenas saw powerful change as well, delivering equally significant social transformation. An epoch-making era of out-of-the-box thinking and innovative entrepreneurial energy stretched across diverse professions.

This was the decade that Apple and Microsoft started and revolutionized technology. It's hard now to remember life without cell phones, laptops, iPods, Facebook, and word processing and electronic spread sheets. It's the decade that Starbucks altered the way we socialized over coffee; the decade that James Beard and Julia Child transformed the way we thought about the food we ate and how we cooked it. And, it's the decade that the fine wine industry blossomed worldwide. Those of us who decided then to grow wine grapes in Oregon were manifesting that energy. That we created a new industry that reached international acclaim in one generation is a testament to the power of that extraordinary time.

It wasn't easy. Bill worked in Portland during the 1970s and I took part-time jobs locally when I could. My jobs varied from writing for the local paper, teaching American history at Linfield College, and teaching needlepoint at the local yarn store. Besides the practicalities of farming, winemaking, and earning a living, we struggled to have a life as a family. Our solution was to include the kids in whatever we did. We didn't feel we had a choice; there was so much to do. I began to understand why traditional farm families had so many children. Social life, other than mandatory winery events, was reserved for time with grandparents, since both Bill's and my parents had moved to live near us soon after we started the vineyard. Evenings and weekends, until we were able to build a house on the vineyard, we'd drive our pickup up to our property to work until dark. Bill did the heavy work while I drove the tractor with Baby Nik in a backpack. I had envisioned Nik sleeping peacefully with his head on the foam headrest, but that was wishful thinking. He threw off my balance by leaning over the side to peer at what I was doing. Or he cried in my ear.

By the time Alex and Alison were born, we had vineyard help on a daily basis, but our idea of family togetherness stayed the same. We worked in the vineyard, shared chores around the house, or went together to a wine event. The kids learned that work was the norm and their responsibilities increased with age. All three children participated at their level. At winery events, they picked up trash, washed wine glasses, carried cases of wine to buyers' cars and, Alison's favorite, counted the cash box at the end of the day.

Since all time, energy, and funds went into the business, our vacations were minimal, usually camping. Visiting Disneyland had to wait until they took their own children. But the winery gave them other opportunities. When Mt. St. Helens erupted in 1980, Nik and Alex (aged ten and seven) gathered the volcanic ash that landed in the vineyard, bagged it and sold it in our tasting room. I encouraged their budding entrepreneurship. In high school, Nik started a small business chopping and bagging Pinot Noir and Chardonnay grapevine prunings to use as flavoring for barbecuing. Alex helped him collect the canes. After the prunings had dried, the rest of the family, even Bill's parents, came to help. We gathered in our equipment shed, and donned dust masks to help grind, bag, and label our new product. Nik financed his first car with sales of his Grapevine Smoke in our tasting room.

Bill and I had been struggling to make our wine business viable for almost fifteen years when Oregon Pinot Noir finally burst on the national radar in the mid-1980s. By 1985, there were enough Oregon wineries to hire a marketing firm. Oregon wine needed to get the attention of wine writers and wine publications, most of whom were based in New York City. Taking a cue from the popular "Pepsi Challenge," the firm arranged a taste-off at the International Wine Center in Manhattan between the best 1983 Oregon Pinot Noirs and top growth French Burgundies of the same vintage. The Oregon vintners carefully selected the wines to represent them. The International Wine Center chose the Burgundian wines. This cheeky move on Oregon's part could be a serious setback if Oregon wines didn't show well. The president of the International Wine Center, who was also a prominent New York wine retailer, advised against the tasting as a poor marketing ploy. He was certain Oregon would not fare well against Burgundy.

Bill was chosen to represent Oregon at the event in mid-September. Since I was managing the vineyard, I stayed home to monitor the crop. Shortly before he left, the two of us walked in the vineyard to look at the grapes and stood in the midst of a block of our Pinot Noir. Bathed in the warmth of a perfect autumn day, we looked out over the lush green canopy, overflowing with clusters of purple grapes ripening in the sun.

"Should we even bother to harvest the crop this year?" I asked, dejected at the thought of leaving such beautiful fruit to rot on the vine. Our Pinot Noir, priced at $7.95 a bottle, was selling so poorly that, at the current rate of sales, we had a three year supply in inventory. Bill shrugged his shoulders.

"Let's see what happens at the tasting," he said. "We can postpone the decision for another week."

I didn't have to be there to imagine exactly how the tasting would go. As a formal seated tasting, rather than a chatty, walk-around affair, Manhattan's premium palates (almost exclusively male) would sit in front of two rows of glasses, each with an ounce of unidentified Pinot Noir wine. This was called a "blind tasting." They would be asked to identify whether the wines were from France or Oregon and then rank their top five favorites. After everyone had finished and voted, the names of the wines would be revealed and discussed. No talking was allowed once the tasting began.

In choreographed sequence, each taster would pick up the first glass, hold it up to the light, then against the white tablecloth to check for color. Next he would swirl the wine to release aromas, and stick his nose into the glass to inhale the bouquet. Only then the first sip, noisily sucking in air at the same time and holding the wine in the mouth to get the full sensation. The timing sequence faltered then as each taster would take a varying amount of time with every wine, to get the full "mouth feel." The last step was to spit out the wine into a cup or spittoon, experience how it finished, and think about it for a moment. Often tasters closed their eyes or stared off into space to connect with the "Zen" of the wine. Finally, they would record their impressions on a notepad. Tasting wine is a skill and spitting it out, rather than swallowing, is obligatory. So often, consumers seem reluctant to spit, thinking it isn't polite. I learned to tell visitors to Sokol Blosser that spitting was the sign of a professional taster.

The same sequence of steps would be repeated with each glass. For forty-five minutes, as tasters sniffed, swirled, sipped, and spit their way through all the wines, the only sounds would be the slurping of wine and the scratching of pencils on the notepads. A winey fragrance would soon envelope the room.

Everyone expected the French wine would come out on top. How could Oregon Pinot Noir begin to compare to wine from the Mother Lode? When the votes were tallied and announced, no one could believe it. To the astonishment of the tasters and the incredulity of the Oregon winemakers who were watching, Oregon swept the competition. Not only were the five favorites from Oregon, but the top tasters of the wine world couldn't tell a French Burgundy from an Oregon Pinot Noir. Sokol Blosser fared exceptionally well, having made the top two wines.

"Extraordinary," one chortled, when an Oregon wine was uncovered. "I was sure it was French." Even before Twitter, the buzz this tasting created could be heard from coast to coast. The results of the tasting set the winery phone ringing; our three year supply sold out in three months. This event marked the start of Oregon Pinot Noir's rise to stardom, although the ascendency we hoped would be immediate, actually took another fifteen years. The decision to wait on whether to pick our grapes turned out to be prudent. Not only did we did harvest our Pinot Noir in October 1985, but that vintage remains my favorite.

The Oregon-Burgundy Challenge did more than help us sell our inventory. Robert Drouhin, from the prominent Burgundian house, Maison Joseph Drouhin, came to Oregon to see the area that had bested France and ended up buying land close to ours. During construction, when Robert and his wife and their winemaker were in Oregon, Bill and I invited them to our winery for lunch. We couldn't entertain such wine royalty with paper plates on our old wooden picnic table so we brought our good china and silverware down to the winery from our house, spread my mother's white damask tablecloth on the picnic table, and sat outside our tasting room under the oak trees for a catered luncheon, awed by the decision of this famous French family to build a winery in Oregon. Drouhin's commitment to Oregon was a major boon to the Oregon wine industry. "There are only two places in the world I would plant Pinot Noir," Robert declared, "Burgundy and Oregon." We cheered this bold statement as affirmation of our long-held belief that Pinot Noir would thrive on Oregon hillsides.

Until the Oregon-Burgundy tasting, Oregon wine was invisible in wine publications. With the spectacular results of the 1985 tasting, Oregon got a small mention in ***The Wine Spectator***, the wine magazine with the largest circulation and influence. It took another twenty-seven years for ***The Wine Spectator*** to echo Robert Drouhin and declare Oregon equal to Burgundy as a Pinot Noir producer. When that happened, in December 2012, many considered it a milestone. We old timers just wondered why it took the ***Spectator*** so long to catch on.

3

Background

While Alex and Alison had trained for the presidency, I took over so suddenly there was no time for training or transition. Until I managed the vineyard, a job I'd been doing since 1980, I had no financial or administrative experience. After leaving high school teaching, a position for which I was trained, I had talked myself into a number of other jobs – manuscripts curator, newspaper reporter, adjunct professor of history. Interviewers looked at my undergraduate degree from Stanford University and graduate degree from Reed College and figured I could do the job.

I took over the vineyard when Bill gave up his day job and came into the winery full time as president. Until then, I went along, working in the winery's tasting room, supporting Bill, and feeling guilty that my enthusiasm did not match his.

Managing the vineyard put me in the field every day, driving the tractor or doing hand work (pruning, suckering, pulling leaves, thinning the crop), and overseeing a small crew. I grew to love the seasonal moods and the rhythm of the vineyard cycle. I had found my place. Watching the vines leaf out every spring, the baby leaves unfurling with rosy tipped edges and miniature grape clusters, never stopped delighting me. I loved the shadows from the early morning sun as I'd walk up a vineyard row, breathing deeply at the smell of freshly worked earth, watching the hawks ride the air currents over the vineyard, and the goldfinches, bluebirds, and swallows flutter among the vines.

At these times, the vineyard and I become one. Caring for the vineyard sparked my passion for our business, a fervor which eventually surpassed Bill's. I could have lived my whole life in the city and never discovered the attachment to the land, the sense of place, that welled up deep inside and became central to my life. For me, the vineyard remains the most engaging, emotionally satisfying part of the wine business.

Immersed in the vines, I was able to forget our winery woes. The general recession of the late 1980s, with its deadly combination of skyrocketing interest rates and sluggish wine sales, compounded the growing pains of the young wine industry. By 1990, Sokol Blosser Winery found itself at a crisis point. We were so strapped for cash we could neither hire help nor buy many grapes for harvest that year. We cut back, using our tasting room staff to process the grapes. Along with the winery's financial distress, Bill's and my personal standard of living had slipped over the past ten years. Every year we had tightened our belts a little more. The pinch was getting unbearable.

"One of us needs to get a real job," I told Bill. It was December 1990. Ten years had passed since Bill had taken over as president. We had rented a house at the coast with the extended family to celebrate Christmas. We left the house to walk along the beach to talk, braving the cold wet wind. It was the first time we had taken a hard look at our situation. "We can't go on like this," I continued, feeling I had finally put into words what I'd been feeling for way too long.

"You could go back to teaching high school social studies," Bill suggested. I stopped walking and looked at him, trying to decide if that was a quip or if he was serious. Seeing how drained and beaten down he looked, a pang of guilt swept over me. I should do more, be the one to get another job.

"Yes, I guess I could," I said, yet going back to teaching was a terrible thought. My heart felt heavy just thinking about creating lesson plans, grading illegible papers, and trying to keep control of a roomful of high school students whose hormones were on fast forward while their brains were on hold. Yet I had been a teacher and had only to renew my teaching certificate.

Then I realized my hesitation included something else. After being the decision-maker for the vineyard for ten years, I had discovered I liked working for myself. It wasn't less work. Being the boss made me work harder, feeling I had to set an example. Nor was the type of work the issue. I simply chafed at the thought of working for someone else. Also, although I deplored it, Bill could command a much higher salary in the marketplace. It really made more sense for him to get an outside job.

"Would you consider going back to planning?" I asked. He

was squinting against the wind, but as he raised his eyebrows at my suggestion, I thought I saw a flicker of hope cross his face.

"Yes," he said, sounding surprised at his answer. We had been standing alone on the windswept beach, facing each other during those three minutes of conversation. A moment of silence hung between us as we each let our words sink in. Then, as if a light bulb went off, the conversation suddenly took a 180 degree turn. Once Bill admitted he had lost his passion for the winery, the solution fell into place, a surprise neither of us could have predicted. Before the holiday ended, Bill had called our partners together to tell them.

Just a week later, on January 2, 1991, Bill announced, at a hastily called meeting with our partners, that I would take over as President of Sokol Blosser Winery. The decision was sudden, although Bill's leaving wasn't unexpected. They knew how burned out he was. The surprise was my taking over, and our partners turned to me with new eyes, curious and wary. They knew me as a vineyard manager; winery president implied a shift in focus and priorities. What won them over was that I was willing to work for half Bill's salary, far less than if they hired an experienced person. Equally important, Bill and I only owned half the business. They would keep me on a short leash.

If I had been an outsider with no formal financial or administrative training, I would never have been hired. My master's degree was for teaching, not business. Hiring me may not have been the best business decision, but it was my chance and I grabbed it.

I don't know what made me think I could run a business, especially one as troubled as ours. But finally passionate about our enterprise, I found myself eager to jump into the mess I had inherited. As a woman, my position as President of Sokol Blosser was virtually unique at the time.

Women traditionally took support roles in the wine industry, as in most agricultural and processing enterprises in the late 20th century. This doesn't diminish the hard work and importance to the development of the Oregon wine industry of women like Nancy Ponzi, Diana Lett, Ginny Adelsheim, Virginia Fuller, or Kina Erath. Each one worked tirelessly and had significant input at their vineyard and winery. But they were not the first string, not the decision makers. Wives were the bench; husbands the starters. Despite their lesser role, as so often happens, the bench was critical to winning the game. But the focus was on the guys. Early publicity photos featured men only; one wouldn't have guessed how important wives were. Years later, Bill admitted the founders looked at themselves as a men's club. Proving the point, Dick Erath entitled his memoir, ***The Boys Up North***. That the wives were invisible was a sign of the times, before the women's movement changed the playing field.

I relished the challenge, excited to be a female decision-maker in a male industry. My three older brothers had taught me to be at ease with men and I considered it a test, as a woman, to succeed in the male wine world.

There was no transition period. After a brief respite, Bill went back to work in Portland at the large engineering-planning firm he had left ten years earlier to come full-time into the winery. They were glad to have him back and called his decade away his sabbatical. Re-energized, he soon rose to become head of the firm's Portland office.

It was as if Bill handed me the key and disappeared. On January 3rd, as I sat in his former President's chair and looked around his former office, I realized I now had power, but no knowledge. I didn't even know where anything was and spent my first days looking through drawers and file cabinets to see what was there.

As I moved up from bench to starter, a dormant entrepreneurial drive surfaced from deep inside, spurring me on. Petrified but exhilarated, I took over the presidency of Sokol Blosser Winery at age forty-six, slowly growing into my role. Now, I look back with wonderment. This was never anything I ever imagined doing. Not that I didn't have wild dreams, but running a vineyard and winery was never in the mix. I was neither a farm girl, wine geek, nor business person.

My only claim to farm life is that when I was born, in 1944, my parents, Phyllis and Gus Sokol, lived at Melody Farm, in Waukesha, Wisconsin. In 1942, to combat the austerity measures of World War Two, they gave up the city life they had always known and moved with my three brothers to the country, where they could raise their own meat and grow their own food. Their picture book farm life, with its whitewashed brick farmhouse and barns, bordered by a split rail fence, lasted only seven years, but it loomed large in our family lore.

Family stories of my mother driving a horse and buggy to the local store during wartime gas rationing and my father keeping chickens, pigs, and horses, kept the memory alive, but my personal knowledge of farm life was meager. By the time I was four, we had moved back to the city. I grew up as an upper middle class urbanite. My early memories include helping my father choose the right patterned silk tie to go with his suit every morning; listening to my parents talk about the theater and concerts; the smell of my mother's perfume and tickle of her fur coat as she leaned down to kiss me after coming home late from an evening out. I can't imagine either of them harnessing a horse or mucking out a chicken coop.

One year, long after we had our own families, my three older brothers and I visited Mother and Daddy at the same time. As we sat around talking, we got the idea of driving out to see if the farm that lived in our imaginations was still there. On impulse, the four of us jumped in the car and headed out. What had been farmland had become a sea of housing developments. We found the old house, reduced to a large lot, a little oasis tucked among town houses and condos. The Melody Farm sign, grown shabby through the years, still swung in the breeze above the weathered split rail fence.

We stood silently at first, gazing at the sea of identical houses with square front lawns and parallel driveways that made our old brick farmhouse look out of place. When we compared memories, only my oldest brother, Jerry, in his early teens when I was born, could remember the farmland of the 1940s, and riding his horse through the nearby fields. Henry, next in line, remembered the local schoolhouse.

"Little Dixon School," he remembered. "Eight rows, eight grades." Ronnie, the youngest brother, five years older than I, spoke of his dog, a collie named Beauty, a gift to him at my birth. Closing my eyes, I could see myself sitting alone on the edge of the sandbox in the front yard, scooping sand into a pail with a small shovel, dressed in my blue "Clad-easy," a one piece child's jumpsuit popular at the time. I may have been born on a farm, but I was not a farm girl. There was nothing in my childhood that presaged my future driving a tractor, starting a family farming business, and feeling a deep connection to the land.

Once the family moved to Whitefish Bay, on the east side of Milwaukee, I started kindergarten at the local public school. My birthday was after the cut-off date for entering and my mother liked to tell the story of how she went to the principal to argue that I should be allowed to enroll early, as I was so mature. She won (which is why she liked to tell the story) and I started as the youngest student in the class, a position I held throughout my schooling. I don't know whether I was as "mature" as my mother alleged, but being the youngest never bothered me. As the youngest at home, it was a role I knew. I learned if I paid attention and worked hard, it didn't matter how old I was. As I rose to the top of the class academically, being the youngest became a badge of honor.

The home I grew up in, where my family lived from the time I was four until after I was married, was a large, twenty-six room, 1920s Tudor revival house. I loved that house and still wander through it in my mind, entering through the heavy wooden double front door into the large wood paneled front hall with its black-and-white parquet marble floor. The other rooms opened off the front hall. It could have been the model for the board game ***Clue***.

Each room conveyed its own character. Mother's grand piano graced the "sun room," a windowed half circle off the living room. The wood paneled library walls were floor to ceiling bookshelves. With its gray stone fireplace and giant library table, it radiated learning. A leather wingback chair was perfect for reading. My father, surprisingly well-read with no university degree, loved George Bernard Shaw; we had at least four different leather bound sets of his works. We also had an Encyclopedia Britannica, eight feet of impressive leather tomes, as well as volumes of poems, biographies, and memoirs.

We called this room "the Study," and it became that for me. My brother Ronnie became my taskmaster when he took a professorial interest in my education. I don't know how he did it, but he got me to memorize poems by 19th century Americans, William Cullen Bryant, Henry Wadsworth Longfellow, and James Greenleaf Whittier. His commanding manner scared me, but it worked. I still can recite most of the poems.

He also took on the role of literary police. One time, in the early 1950s, as I sat happily absorbed in a new Nancy Drew mystery story, he snatched the book from me. When I cried out, he handed me a volume of Sherlock Holmes.

"Get rid of that Nancy Drew rubbish," he said. "If you like mysteries, here's what you ought to read."

I stopped crying and started to read the book he had handed me. It drew me in immediately. I never went back to Nancy Drew, but her independent fearless spirit, her girlfriends, Bess and George, her roadster and her adventures, gave her an icon status that Sherlock Holmes couldn't dislodge. I was dismayed to learn years later that author Carolyn Keene was a pseudonym for a series of formula writers who were hired by the publisher to carry on the storyline.

Home from college one summer, Ronnie also took time to read Shakespeare with me. I only agreed because I liked the attention. We sat in the Study and took turns reading Hamlet out loud. When I read a phrase, it sounded dry and stilted. But when Ronnie explained it and read it dramatically, the story came to life. He was more like a father than a brother. His interest and willingness to teach me satisfied my longing for attention and stimulated my intellectual curiosity. I looked up to him and was always ready to do his bidding. The downside of our relationship was that for many years I let him dominate me. Long into adulthood, when I was able to hold my own, our relationship grew closer and more equal.

I saw my other brothers, Henry, ten years older, and Jerry, thirteen years older, mostly on holidays and summers. I barely knew Jerry, who left for college when I was five. Being so much younger, and the only girl, besides my time with Ronnie, I grew up with the loneliness of an only child. The children's books I loved, like ***Little Women*** and ***Little House in the Big Woods***, made me wish I had at least one sister.

Growing up with older brothers, I've always been comfortable around males. They were around enough that seeing them in their underwear, talking about sports, watching football or tennis on TV, or just nonstop brotherly teasing, seemed perfectly normal. As a result, I've usually felt more at ease with men than women. Navigating the male business world or being the only woman at business meetings seemed natural.

My mother represented the conventional female role, standing steadfastly behind my father. When he supported the vineyard, she did too. She let Daddy control the business world and turned her quest for power towards her children. She encouraged me to apply for an American Field Service (AFS) student exchange my junior year in high school. When I was accepted and assigned to Japan, my father said, "Absolutely not! It's too far away." I dissolved in tears at his pronouncement, not yet savvy enough to know that, even if he didn't pay much attention to me, my father didn't want me very far from home. My mother whispered, "You'll go. Don't worry." She stood up for me again when I was accepted on early admissions to Stanford University and my father said, "She can't go there, it's too far away." This time I knew from experience what to expect and looked to my mother. She smiled, "You'll go." Underneath a thick layer of decorum, my stay-at-home mom was a feminist.

The independence she encouraged came as a mixed message since she wanted particulars on everything I did. Nor did she hesitate to pass judgment when I told her. She didn't even have to speak; she gave me her opinion with a look. What I wore, how I fixed my hair, who I was with and, once I had children, how I raised them. It was more advice than I wanted. I usually gave in or brushed off her requests, mainly to maintain peace. On the few occasions I protested her interfering, she defended herself, "I only want what's best for you." Occasionally I find myself telling my children what they "should" do. They're not as timid as I was and let me know I've crossed the line with them. I apologize and tell them I'm channeling my mother.

My father wore a suit, with a silk tie and fedora to work every day. Business was his life. He could not have imagined, when he bought a tannery and started his own company in Milwaukee, Wisconsin, in the early 1950s, that his success would make it possible for his daughter to start a winery in Dayton, Oregon, twenty years later.

I grew up with the smell of leather. General Split, my father's company, processed the underside of a cowhide, called the split. Separated horizontally, the top was the grain; the bottom, or split, was used mainly to make sturdy work gloves. Tanning was a malodorous business and the smell permeated my childhood. The distinctive aroma of tannic acid emanated from the suits my father wore to his office and the car he drove. Even now, I don't shrink from the smell. Entering a car with new leather seats, I inhale nostalgia and memories.

My father was adamant about not bringing work home, but talk at the family dinner table always began with the latest news from my father's tannery. My mother and I listened. By his emphasis and body language, we understood my father was talking to his sons, not to his wife or daughter. The unspoken message that business was man's work came through loud and clear. That was okay with me. Business talk about negotiating sales contracts, strike threats, or sales figures, bored me. I never suspected I would end up as a business owner. When I decided to hand the winery presidency over to my kids, it struck me that my father, who died before I took over the winery, would have been proud that one of his four children had built a business that achieved an international reputation and was being handed down to the next generation. But he would have been surprised that the child who did it was his only daughter.

I have pondered whether entrepreneurship is a nature or nurture phenomenon. My brothers and I chose different paths, but we all followed our father and ran our own businesses. My three children have done the same. I thought that Nik, Alex, and Alison would run away from owning their own business after seeing Bill and me work and worry so much. I see now that they grew up accepting hard work, risk, and tension as a part of life. Each seems to be a born entrepreneur.

My father was forty-five when I was born, a girl after three boys. I never doubted his love for me, but felt a certain unease, as if he didn't quite know what to say to a daughter. Although he sometimes drove me to school, he never participated in parent-teacher conferences, or came to school performances. I can still recall the awkwardness of the one school activity we did together when he went with me on our school's father-daughter field trip to a Milwaukee Braves baseball game. He was not a baseball fan and had taken the afternoon off work to come, probably at my mother's insistence. I can imagine her admonishing him, "Gus, you have to go with Susie on this field trip. It's only one time, all her friends' fathers are going, and she doesn't want to be left out."

We climbed onto the big yellow school bus, along with the other father-daughter pairs. As we bumped along through Milwaukee's industrial district to the baseball stadium, I watched the others talking and laughing. Everyone seemed to be chattering except us. I didn't have the easy repartee with my father that my brothers had and wasn't used to doing things alone with my father without the rest of the family, or at least my mother. Daddy and I sat silently while I tried to think of something to say. I felt responsible and wanted him to enjoy being with me, but the more I stressed, the more tongue-tied I got. I remember nothing about the Braves' game, which would have featured baseball greats Hank Aaron, Warren Spahn, and Eddie Mathews. The uncomfortable bus ride trumped everything else.

My good memories revolve around meals. My father was an epicure. We ate well at home; Mother kept sides of beef, pork, and lamb in the freezer. Summers, on the way home from golf, he'd stop at a local farm and bring home a dozen ears of fresh-picked corn for that night's dinner, then urge those of us around the table to finish them all. Slathered with butter and salt, my brothers often ate three ears apiece. He took us out for dinner regularly, often downtown to Karl Ratsch's, Milwaukee's finest, where the trio of musicians in German frocks and lederhosen fiddled their way around the dining room, and the wiener schnitzel, salted rye rolls, and strawberry schaumtorte were legendary. For more exotic fare, we went to Ming Gardens, Milwaukee's premier (perhaps only) Chinese restaurant. Chinese in those days meant Cantonese – egg foo yung, egg rolls, and chicken chow mein.

When his business took him to France, he expanded his repertoire to French cuisine and French wine. He was fascinated with France's regional cuisine, and shared special tidbits of knowledge with the family; like how interesting it was that the northern part of France used butter while the southern part used olive oil. Daddy introduced me to A.J. Liebling's food essays, which remain, for me, the gold standard of food writing.

He started collecting top growth French and German wines, procured from a local wine merchant. Since mixed drinks were the norm among my parents' social set, and Milwaukee was the home of major breweries at the time, my father's interest in wine was atypical. He created a wine cellar in the basement, claiming a large closet at the base of the stairs of our old house, between the laundry and the furnace rooms. Just living with him, I absorbed his entrepreneurial spirit, his love of good food, and his interest in wine.

Wine accompanied every dinner and choosing the right wine for the meal an important ritual. Daddy would find out what Mother was cooking and then go down to his wine cellar, consider his inventory, and make a decision. Then he explained to me what he had chosen, his reasoning, and a bit about the vineyard or the vintage. As the only child left at home, I got the benefit of his knowledge. I was in high school and not particularly interested in wine, but I loved the attention.

Without knowing it, and with no sense of the value of his cellar, I developed a palate for fine wine. I think longingly of the wines routinely on our family's dinner table. He was judicious in his pours but never watered it down, just gave me a bit so I could get the full taste. I felt so adult to be included. Chateau Haut Brion, Chateau Lafite, Gevrey-Chambertin, Nuits-Saint-Georges, Puligny-Montrachet, Ockfener Bockstein, Piesporter – Bordeaux, Burgundy, Mosel. These fabulous wines were an everyday part of my childhood.

The remarkable vintages of my father's great wine cellar have receded to distant memory. Occasionally today I will taste a Pinot Noir with the earthiness of those old Burgundies – layered flavors of mushroom, black cherry, and leather, interwoven with a hint of barnyard bouquet – and a picture springs to mind of my father coming up the stairs from the basement, cradling the bottle he has selected for the evening. I am suddenly back sipping wine with my father. He's sitting across from me in his leather chair, holding the wine up to the light to check the color. "This is good, eh?" he says. It's a sweet memory.

About 1980, when my father turned eighty, my mother became perpetually annoyed with him. Because he prided himself on his well tailored clothes, she thought he was deliberately antagonizing her by appearing in bizarre pant and shirt combinations. They had just moved to McMinnville, Oregon, seven miles from Bill and me and the vineyard, so I got to see this for myself. Within a few years, Daddy's inexplicable behavior was prominent enough to command the whole family's attention. He didn't acknowledge it or seem aware of it, but something was clearly wrong. Mother and I found a clinic in downtown Portland that specialized in tests for dementia and a disease that had started appearing in the news, called Alzheimer's. They gave him a series of verbal tests to determine which part of the brain was responding, then told us my father had Alzheimer's disease, for which there was no cure. His behavior would continue to deteriorate; at some point he would be unable to care for himself.

Mother's annoyance turned into concern, and the family watched as he departed, little by little, over the next years. Bedridden, his brain uninhabited by memory, sense of purpose, or any cognitive function, he died in a nursing home in March 1988, of pneumonia, a gift, considering his advanced Alzheimer's.

The night he died, Mother called me just after midnight to say the care home had called her; Daddy wouldn't live much longer and if we wanted to be with him we needed to go right away. I dimly remember getting dressed, driving in the black of night the fifteen minutes to her house, then another twenty minutes to the nursing home. A nurse met us at the door of the darkened building and we rushed to his room. We were too late. He lay, with his head on a pillow, his alabaster skin stretched across his cheeks, his mouth open and toothless. His teeth sat next to his bed in a jar. I made particular note of his mouth because I had never known that he had false teeth.

I thought I would cry. My father had just died, I should be crying. But the will to be strong prevailed. I told myself I could cry later. My brothers and their families came for the funeral later that month.

The patriarch of the family, the man who had given us abundance as children, financed our university educations, and passed significant funds to us from the success of his business, had died. The tears didn't come then either. My emotion lay buried.

Because my relationship with my father, while loving, was emotionally distant, I concluded his role had been to provide me a good education and money to start a vineyard, more Daddy Warbucks than Mike Brady of the Brady Bunch. I felt provided for, not nurtured. Now, as I look back at the turns my life has taken, I see how significant his impact has been. My father's effect on my life was more subtle than my mother's, but no less meaningful. I cry now, realizing his profound influence and knowing it's too late to thank him.

With more foresight than we had, Daddy had told Bill and me that the vineyard would be the new family business. I think he was really excited at the thought of our creating a business around something he loved. We were able to buy our first piece of vineyard property with money that had flowed to me from the success of General Split, and he invested personally in our vineyard once he was convinced we were serious. Just as important, he helped us get a loan from the bank he used for his business. This was a godsend as no banks were lending to vineyards then. Wine was an "uncertain enterprise," in the same risky category as restaurants. Daddy encouraged us to keep going and build a winery, pressuring my three brothers to invest in this new family venture, a combination of our family names, Sokol Blosser Winery.

4

Strife

When I took control of the winery, in January 1991, I lived in fear of making some stupid mistake that would highlight my incompetence. I knew how to act self-assured, a veneer I learned as a teenager. My brother Ronnie had told me, when I was in my teens, that if I kept my mouth shut and nodded as if I understood, people would think I was smarter than I was. Since I believed everything he told me, I tried it and found it worked. But during winery board meetings when our partners peppered me with difficult questions, and Bill sat silently by, I would get overwhelmed, frustrated that I wasn't adequately defending myself. I never actually cried at a board meeting, but more than once I wanted to.

One afternoon, following a board meeting, Jack, the winery's financial advisor, dropped by my office. I was feeling particularly discouraged and I guess it showed. He sat down next to me, leaned back in the chair and crossed his legs like he was settling in.

"Something's wrong," he said. "What is it?" His concern opened the floodgate and I confessed how scared I was at winery board meetings when our partners badgered me and I felt like target practice. Jack leaned forward and smiled his friendly smile. I looked forward to his words of sympathy.

"Do you know how pearls are formed?" he asked. "This beautiful jewel is formed by developing a tough covering in the face of aggravation. This is good for you. You are a pearl in formation."

Instead of sympathy, I got tough love. But it reframed my perspective, and his belief in me buoyed my spirit.

Over the course of the 1990s, the winery's financial position stabilized, and I became more self-assured as president. As that happened, I felt more constricted in my marriage. The confidence I felt at the winery dissipated at home where nothing I did seemed to measure up to Bill's standards. I had been trying to meet those standards since we got together. Even the handcrafts I did when the kids were little, in the 1970s and 80s, like macramé, needlepoint, and knitting, suffered from his reaction. "Do you like it?" I'd ask about a needlepoint design I'd spent many hours creating. He'd barely give it a cursory look. Having grown up thinking I was not artistic, his response reinforced my self-doubt. Even as I got more advanced and taught needlepoint at a local knitting store in the late 1970s, Bill treated my work as trivial.

My teenage dream of being cherished remained unfulfilled, buried deep inside. I wasn't good enough, neither sufficiently attractive nor vivacious, to deserve being loved. Bill wanted me to lose weight; I could feel his disapproval whenever I ate. He tried to stop criticizing me, but I had already internalized his disapproval and felt it even when he didn't intend it. Unlike me, always hungry and fighting weight, Bill was the opposite. He didn't understand that food was my attempt to nurture myself. But then, neither did I.

"If you're hungry," he'd say, "have a glass of water."

For years I accepted that it was my fault that I wasn't everything Bill wanted me to be. I suspect my internal criticizing predated Bill; he reinforced the negative self image I already had. That image slowly started to change as my success running the winery gave me newfound confidence. When I began to think that maybe I was worthy, Bill's criticism started to sound hollow. Maybe it was about him, not me.

In the summer of 1993, almost three years after I had become President, I decided to leave the marriage. I blamed Bill for belittling me and never wanted to speak to him again. The friend I went to stay with consoled me but urged me to keep communication open. "Whatever you do, don't stop talking to him."

I had never lived alone, moving from my parents' home, to a college dorm, then right into marriage. Like other women of my generation, I was taught to feel incomplete without a man. Living alone frightened me. As my anger subsided, I was lonely; I missed family life. The little apartment I rented started off as refuge and evolved into punishment. Bill took me back and we agreed to see a marriage counselor and work on our relationship. Discovering I was part of the problem, and that I had let Bill control me, undercut the self-pity I had cultivated. I would have preferred to blame Bill for my unhappiness and the failure of our marriage.

Five years later, I left again. This time the break was thoughtful, solemn, and final, a measure of how much more confident I had become. We sat in the lobby bar at The Benson, Portland's grand old hotel with its expansive lobby, its plush chairs and dark wood paneling capturing the ambiance of a former era. We faced each other over a glass of wine, admitting things each had kept hidden for years. It was honest communication, but it had come too late. Bill asked me to stay but, his eyes held a hesitancy and I could tell his heart wasn't in it. Deep down, he knew the marriage was over. We'd been together thirty-two years.

At fifty-four years old, I told myself I would probably be alone the rest of my life. The chances of finding someone at my age were slim. I telephoned my mother to tell her, expecting her, as a strong independent woman, to congratulate me on this huge move I was making. She was silent for a moment before responding.

"You left Bill? Why would you do that? He was a good husband, wasn't he?" Her short exclamations burst through the phone lines. "You won't be invited to parties as a single woman," she went on. I felt like she essentially scolded me, saying that unless Bill were physically abusing me, why wouldn't I stay with him, for my own good?

She demanded details – what had he done? Since my leaving seemed sudden to her, she may have thought there would be a triggering event, like catching him in bed with another woman. I was hurt, then angry, at her reproach and immediately withdrew from the conversation. She apparently couldn't understand that I was trying to put the pieces of myself together. I avoided her for the next two weeks, until she called Alison to ask about me. When I called her, it was clear she had no idea how much she had upset me. She continued to ask me periodically about my decision, and I always changed the subject. She died wondering why I left Bill when he was such a good husband.

As I left home to move into a little apartment, taking only my clothes and my cat, sadness and elation overwhelmed me in turn. I had tried for thirty-two years to be the person Bill wanted me to be. Now I was at liberty to be myself, whoever that was. I hoped I would have the courage to find out.

Bill and I had waited to announce the split to our kids, all of whom were married and in their own homes, right after Christmas, 1998. We wanted one last family Christmas together. I thought they would take the news in stride. Big miscalculation. What had been foremost in my world caught them unaware. I had kept my unhappiness so well hidden that my kids hadn't seen it. They saw their Mom as her usual jovial self, so Bill's and my parting was a huge and unwelcome surprise. They were shocked, upset, indignant, and wanted to meet with me to discuss what they saw as a precipitous act.

We met at Nik's home. It was just me and my three adult children, sitting uneasily in the living room of Nik's small house. I could feel the sadness in the air. Across the room, Nik looked at me with sorrowful eyes and rocked slowly back and forth in his chair, a nervous habit from childhood. Standing behind my chair, Alex put his arm around me in sympathy. Seated at the other end of the couch, Alison twisted a lock of hair and confronted me. Why did I leave Dad?

I didn't know what to say. I didn't want to make Bill out as the bad guy. He was their father. I couldn't tell them I wanted to get out from under Bill's emotional control, a control I had submitted to. Yet their sad faces made me want to explain. I mumbled something about my needing to find myself and heard myself flounder. Rather than say my leaving Bill was a move of growth and courage, I took the blame for breaking up the family. What I saw as liberation came across as a selfish act.

I've often wondered what would have happened if I had just said what was in my heart; if I had been willing to be more open and able to explain the dynamics of our marriage. In a time of evolution of male-female relations, an honest explanation might have helped my children deal with their own marriages. As their models for male-female relations, our coming unglued did more than break up the family. Nik told me later that Bill's and my separation had come at a time he was examining his role in his own marriage. The breakup of a relationship he saw as solid unnerved him. Nor did I know that Alex and Alison were each struggling in their marriages.

Preoccupied with my own unhappiness, I hadn't considered how my leaving their father would shatter their world, threaten their sense of security, and untangle the threads that held us together even though they were adults and had left home. I also underestimated the strength of my own ties to the family. Christmas and other family rituals were never the same. Leaving Bill generated a tough emotional tradeoff. In my attempt to find myself, I had destroyed the family element that was one of my core values. A deep sadness over that unraveling remains.

With the passage of time I began to understand the complexities of Bill's and my relationship. My outward feminism was ardent and genuine. But buried deep beneath lurked fears of abandonment. The way to survive was to yield, even if it meant eclipsing myself. I had surrendered my power to Bill, just as I had earlier to my mother. Outwardly strident and inwardly submissive, the only way to become a whole person was to leave. Recognizing primal fears at the core of my being has not extinguished them, but exposing them to the light has had a diminishing effect.

It took several years for Bill's and my separate wounds to heal. Concern for our children and being together on the winery board of directors kept us in touch. A heartfelt connection developed over the years, both of us admitting that the ties from our thirty-two years of marriage, three children, who were the center of our lives, and taking a business through hard times, bound us together in ways neither of us would ever have with anyone else.

"I want you at my bedside when I die," I blurted out when we met for lunch in 2011, shortly before he remarried, to a woman I liked a lot. We were sitting at a table for two at a Vietnamese restaurant, waiting for our stir fried vegetables and noodles. It was such an odd thing to say and it came out before I could censor it. Bill looked surprised, then he sighed softly. "Yeah, I'll be there," he said. "If you'll be at mine." Calling each other periodically to discuss winery or family issues, we never identified ourselves. "Hi, it's me," sufficed. At winery board meetings he and I often viewed issues from the same perspective, reflecting our experience and probably our generation.

At the time, however, leaving Bill dealt me an unanticipated financial blow. The act of divorce immediately put all our property into a fifty-fifty balance, regardless of previous ownership. As a married woman, I had owned 75 percent of the vineyards and 62 percent of the winery. Filing for divorce immediately lowered both percentages to 50 percent. To regain a controlling share of the business, I had to trade all the other assets. I was willing to give up my share of our house, our furnishings, our art, as well as any investments in my name. My new freedom had unleashed a fierce desire to own both the vineyard and the winery.

Bill and I divvied up our property in about two weeks, and then left it in the hands of our attorneys who thrashed about for more than a year. When it was all over, I had little else, but the business was essentially mine. I was majority owner of both the vineyard and the winery.

I felt at the top of my game, enjoyed being President, and relished my command. After sharing ownership control for almost thirty years, it felt good to be on my own. I started to explore all the options – selling, taking in investors, or keep going with our family.

When my father had declared, back when we first started, that the winery would be the new family business, I didn't think much about it. Bill and I were doing our thing. Our kids were little. What having a family business meant wasn't a big concern. After Bill and I formally divorced, and the five of us (Bill, the three kids and myself) got together for a winery board meeting, I casually floated the idea of selling the winery. I was flexing my owner's muscle and thinking about the possibilities. Shocked faces from my kids told me how strongly all three felt about keeping it.

Nik, Alex, and Alison were not only unanimous, they were vehement about keeping the winery in the family. The strength of their reaction surprised me. They grew up with the vineyard and winery part of their lives, but Bill and I never talked to them about joining us. It was a hard life. I had assumed that seeing their parents' struggle would have made them want to leave, but that wasn't the case. Our oldest son, Nik, said he didn't want to give up such an important part of his childhood. He had good memories of driving the tractor, picking cherries when we still had orchards and selling them to winery visitors, building a giant tree house, and generally roaming the vineyard. Nik demonstrated his own entrepreneurial gene when he started his own business in Portland, Celilo Group Media, a media company to expand the market for sustainable products. But his emotional ties to the vineyard and winery hadn't waned. His heart was at the vineyard although he had to live in Portland.

Alex, the middle child, had gone off to college in San Antonio, Texas, without any specific goals, ready to follow whatever caught his fancy, starting with a major in philosophy. Within a year, he realized that the vineyard was in his blood. He missed it enough that he transferred to Oregon State University, then left school to work, first at a neighboring vineyard and then for a Portland wine distributor. In 1998, I talked him into coming to work for me to help with sales. At the time, I was fully engaged in instituting my vision of Sokol Blosser's renaissance and thinking only of the immediate future; I needed his help. Alex was then twenty-four, adept at setting up grocery store Snapple displays, and just learning the wine business. After joining me, he finished college and attended night school at Portland State University to get his MBA. Alex and his wife built a house at the base of the vineyard so their twin boys could grow up as Alex did, close to the earth, among the vines. He definitely didn't want to sell.

My youngest child and only daughter, Alison, six years younger than Alex, had spent her last year of high school studying in France, then decided to stay home, attend Portland State University, and get married. She worked part-time for me while she was in school. Her organizational prowess and capacity for thinking ahead made her a valuable assistant. I discovered she liked to try out my chair when I wasn't there. Once, I returned and found her sitting at my desk. She swiveled around when I came charging in, stopping with surprise when I saw her at my desk. I looked at her as I put my briefcase down, wondering if she was thinking about her future. As she slowly relinquished my seat, I asked.

"What role do you see for yourself at the winery?" She didn't hesitate.

"Your position," she said with a grin. She was barely twenty.

After graduation, she worked for me for a while, then decided she too needed an MBA and went off to the University of Washington for two years, renting an apartment, and commuting back to Portland on weekends, toting her cat in a carrier next to her. She didn't want to sell the winery.

As the majority stockowner, I could have pushed for another option, but the idea of selling didn't appeal to me either. I was just floating different options as they occurred to me. Positioned at the helm, and in full ownership control, I was ready to lead the family business forward. I had already hired an experienced winemaker to take the winery to the next level of quality.

When Bill stepped out of my daily life in 1998, an unexpected player stepped in. Earlier that year, I had decided we needed to change winemakers. I wanted not merely an experienced commercial winemaker, but one who had worked with Pinot Noir and Oregon grapes. Most Oregon winemakers were still self-taught. To find the skill level I wanted, I needed to look to California. I thought of Russ Rosner whom Bill had hired in the 1980s to consult on our barrel program. Russ had been a senior enologist with Robert Mondavi Winery when he consulted with us. Here was someone who knew Sokol Blosser and had the requisite skills and experience. I looked him up to see if he would be interested and discovered he was in-between jobs, undecided where to go next.

A month later, I flew down to Napa to interview him. I stayed with my friend, Eugenia; Russ came to her house for the interview. Russ was short, barely my height, fit and athletic looking. My first impression was that everything about him seemed carefully considered. His beard and mustache were well designed and closely trimmed. He spoke slowly, thoughtfully. He wore a serious, almost stern expression.

"I just want to make wine," he told me quietly. "I have no desire to own a winery and deal with all the issues ownership entails." This was key, since winemakers who had made several Oregon wineries famous had recently left to start their own operations. Russ's references talked about his integrity, his attention to detail, his total focus on quality. Not a winemaker myself, I needed someone with those qualities whom I could trust. In return I would give him almost complete freedom to do the job.

A successful winemaker needs a delicate balance between left and right brain, between science and intuition. Great chefs require the same. Both need technical aptitude combined with creativity to make the right intuitive judgment call at critical moments, whether it's knowing the seasoning that will lift a dish from good to sensational or deciding the moment to cut back the pressure when pressing Pinot Noir so the wine has just the right balance. Both professions are full of such critical moments.

But winemaking offers a unique twist. Since wine grapes ripen once a year, each harvest constituting a vintage, a winemaker gets only one chance a year to make wine. Thirty vintages constitute a long winemaking career. Compare that to a chef who could create meals every day of the year. A chef gets immediate feedback from diners and can adjust or just do the same thing for the next meal. A winemaker lets the new Pinot Noir wine rest in barrels for twelve to eighteen months before bottling, and then ages it further before releasing it for sale. Think of the pressure each harvest, knowing it's your only chance to make wine that year, then the deferred gratification required, having to wait years before your creation is mature.

Both passion and patience are needed to make great wine. I

will never be a winemaker, but I know what it takes and am full of admiration for those who do it well. I convinced Russ that he would have complete control over the winemaking at Sokol Blosser and the opportunity to make great Pinot Noir. He started in July of 1998, the same month as Alex. I was excited to be working with my son. I had no idea that Russ would play an additional role in my life.

Russ and I worked well together from the start, respecting the other for qualities and abilities lacking in ourselves. My vision drew the big picture. He colored it in and made it real. Together, we developed a better way to designate our Pinot Noir bottlings, created new proprietary wine blends, and embarked on a drive towards sustainability across the operation.

The winery production area was built into a rocky knoll, the top side of which led to the tasting room and offices. My office was on the second floor of a building attached to the upper side. Going into the cellar meant going down three flights of stairs, far away enough that I had to make an effort to go to the winery production area. I spent most of my time in the offices, tasting room, and vineyard. But when Russ came on, I became more involved in production. He welcomed me in the cellar, as the previous winemaker had not, patiently answering all my wine production questions, and explaining them clearly enough for my nonscientific brain to follow. He kept me informed of every aspect of each vintage. He taught me the complexities of winemaking and the difficult logistics demanded by our mix of wines.

I liked his approach. Serious and businesslike, he was just what I wanted in a winemaker. His passion for environmental sustainability surpassed my own. He willingly took on the huge task of shepherding our new underground barrel cellar through design, production, and LEED certification (LEED is the U.S. Green Building Council's sustainability accreditation). He helped me find sustainable solutions to operational dilemmas. I was his boss, but it felt more like a partnership.

With no family or friends around, Russ seemed alone all the time. I couldn't tell if he was just introverted or a serious hermit but, since I had brought him to Oregon, I felt some responsibility to help him socialize. After Bill and I separated, when I wanted company at events, I invited Russ to come along. As we spent more time together, I discovered his sternness was a façade. Behind lay a droll sense of humor and a tender heart. When he let me into his world, we connected on an emotional level new to me. We were kindred spirits.

What happened next flew against all proper business protocol and would have raised my eyebrows if I heard it about someone else: I fell in love with Russ. My friend Heidi told me that I was on the rebound, that I should wait at least a year before getting into another relationship. "Be careful. Russ is like a warm bath after being out in the cold," she said. I had been lonely for years. If Russ were a warm bath, I wanted to camp out in the tub.

Not a hermit, but definitely a loner, Russ had never been in a long term relationship. Not letting himself care too much kept him from getting hurt. It took time for him to open his heart and let me in. When that happened, giddy with yearning, we entered a period of intense energy and passion. He was forty-eight and I was fifty-four, but we had the fervor of twenty-year-olds. Entwined in each other's arms at my small Portland apartment, we were two lonely souls who had found each other. The invasive sounds of police sirens and street people rattling their shopping carts of worldly goods down the sidewalk didn't faze us. I felt our spirits merge along with our bodies. Then a horrible thought hit me: here I was trying to find myself and immediately wanting to merge with another. It came as a revelation that I didn't have to give up who I was to have a close relationship. I could still be myself, although I wasn't entirely sure yet who that was.

At five in the morning, when the alarm went off, Russ drove back to his rented house to shower, eat, and get to the winery for work. I went to the gym down the street, then drove the hour to the winery. We lived on the adrenalin of early love. Our serious, all-business veneers helped us keep our feelings out of the workplace; my concern that our new relationship would hinder working together evaporated. Nothing changed. As our relationship became public, the rest of the staff seemed to accept it. At least they didn't say anything to me directly.

My children didn't feel that constraint and probably said what the staff had been thinking. I could tell Alison had been suspicious, calling to check in with me and ask what I was doing. I stopped answering the phone to avoid her questions, but she finally pinned me down and got me to admit what was going on with Russ. She wasn't happy about it. "What does this mean for the winery, Mom?" Though they may have given up hope that I would reconcile with their father, they weren't ready to accept a new face, particularly the face of a winery employee. The local wine world enjoyed spreading the news that

Susan Sokol Blosser had taken up with her winemaker. I didn't care about providing such juicy gossip because I was reveling in newfound joy. At the end of the year, twelve months after I had left Bill, Russ and I had moved out of our individual rentals and bought a house together, halfway between the winery and Portland.

5

Transition Decisions

One morning in January 2004, as another gray Oregon winter day began, I answered my office phone to hear a voice on the other end ask me if I would be available to attend the University of Portland's graduation weekend in May to receive an honorary doctorate. An honorary doctorate? This must be somebody's idea of a joke. When the university spokesman, Brian Doyle, finally convinced me that this was no crank call, I had to ask, "Why me?"

"We've been watching you," Brian said. I didn't respond, waiting for him to explain. "You exemplify qualities we admire and want to promote, especially entrepreneurship within the context of sustainability and community service." Wow. I'd been going along, fixated on what I wanted to accomplish and never thought anyone, especially outside of the wine industry, might be watching. Yet, being a university professor had once been a dream of mine; getting an honorary doctorate would be sweet. "I would be deeply honored," I said, hoping to sound dignified, worthy of such an honor. Then I hung up the phone and twirled around in my office chair. It was all I could do to keep from jumping up and shouting "Yippee!"

I was in my prime. Russ was making our wines better than ever. We were riding a wave of success with a new proprietary blend called Evolution No. 9 (which eventually became just Evolution); our full acreage was finally planted and the vineyard nearing organic certification. Sokol Blosser was a leader in sustainable practices, both in the vineyard and winery, including being the first winery to achieve the U.S. Green Building Council's hard-to-get LEED certification with our new barrel cellar. Customers across the United States and in key global markets, including Japan and Canada, could buy Sokol Blosser wine in the best stores and restaurants. Pinot Noir had new cachet and ours was considered one of the best. I had almost completed my first book,

At Home in the Vineyard, telling the story of our winery, the creation and growth of the Oregon wine industry, and my personal journey from liberal arts major with no skills to business executive.

I had climbed the mountain I'd set out to climb, and the surprise honorary doctorate felt like icing on the cake. But with reflexes from decades of running a business, I was already asking what's next. We couldn't just coast. A business needs a vision to drive it, and the winery needed a new one. Then it hit me: maybe it shouldn't be mine. Maybe it should come from the next generation.

Over the previous year, some seemingly unrelated incidents had lodged in the back of my mind. Together, they formed a pattern pointing to the need for change. For one thing, fatigue hovered over me. The exhilaration of triumphing over challenges had evolved into weariness. After wanting so fiercely to own and run the winery, and giving up so much to achieve it, I found myself reluctant to take on projects that previously I would have tackled eagerly. A little voice in my head whispered that my reluctance could hold the business back. I tried not to listen. My sense of duty kept me going. But the little voice remained.

On a sales trip to Texas, riding with one of our distributor's sales people, I had a sudden image of how I must look to this young person I was riding with. Glancing sideways at the hip young man driving, I wondered how he would have recounted his day to his spouse. I guessed that he might describe me as the old lady he was assigned to spend the day with. Driving around to meet potential customers, he had numerous wines in his portfolio to sell. I had only a few hours to make him a fan of mine. Someone closer to his age, who could relate as a peer, would have a better chance of connecting. I sensed I was getting too old to be doing this.

Financially, the business was getting more complex and competitive. I wondered if I was the right person to be taking Sokol Blosser to the next stage. Having grown the winery from 20,000 cases to over 60,000, had I reached my level of incompetence, to use a phrase from ***The Peter Principle***? When the wine industry was in its infancy, I had been able to manage, even do well. Maybe it was time for someone with more sophisticated skills to take the company forward.

One sunny morning in July, 2004, I drove into Portland to have lunch with Nik. I had cleared my schedule and looked forward to having time alone with my thoughtful and strategic son. I valued his ideas and opinions. Now in his mid-thirties, with receding hairline, three kids of his own, and a fledgling business, we talked easily and openly. He was so busy I didn't get to see him enough. I smiled to myself as I pulled up to his office to pick him up, remembering the Mother's Day card he sent me when his first child was almost a year old. "Mom," it said. "I had no idea. Love, Nik."

When we arrived at the restaurant and I was backing into a parking space, I sighed and mentioned how tired I was. I meant it as a casual comment but as we were getting out of the car, Nik looked at me, and said sympathetically, "I know. I've been wondering when you would start talking about leaving." I had no idea I'd been so transparent.

Was I the only one who hadn't seen it? I'd always assumed I would run the winery the rest of my life – that I was the only one who could. But Nik's remark made the seemingly unrelated incidents in the back of my mind coalesce. It was time to confront my weariness, my lack of a new vision, my age, and my skill set and determine what was in the best interest of the business. The answer flashed through my mind: I should give up the presidency. It was the next thought that astonished me. I was ready to do it. In my mid-forties when I took over, I was now about to celebrate my sixtieth birthday.

Sixty seemed momentous. The birthday that would thrust me into elderhood carried symbolic value. I wanted to treat passing into a new stage of life with some pomp. Russ did his best to line up my kids for a grand birthday dinner in Portland. One by one, they apologized. My midweek birthday night wouldn't work. How about a Sunday brunch? I was disappointed, and disliked brunches, where I always ate too much, but what could I do? I thought, with some malice, that my mother would have tried guilt, but my kids had busy schedules; I told myself I should be happy they were willing to grant me time the following Sunday. I knew they were sorry to disappoint me. When Nik called on my birthday, he apologized again that he was out of town on my big day.

Russ consoled me by making reservations at Higgins, my favorite Portland restaurant. As we drove into Portland for my birthday dinner, he couldn't help but notice me slumping in my seat, feeling sorry for myself. "I'm sorry your kids aren't available," he said. "Isn't having dinner with just me good enough?" "Yes, of course," I mumbled. But I continued staring out the window.

When we arrived at the restaurant and started following the Maitre D' to our table, I stopped in my tracks. Sitting at the table we were moving towards were six people, deliberately holding menus up in front of their faces. When they lowered them I saw my three kids and their spouses grinning at me. Russ had the biggest grin, knowing he had pulled off the first surprise party I'd ever had. Delight wiped out melancholy the second the menus came down. I got all the pomp I could want that evening.

If I were to give up being President of Sokol Blosser, I needed someone to take my place. My preference would be one of my children, but I wasn't sure that would be the best way to go. Nik, immersed in building his own business, was not an option, but there were two others. Alex and Alison were both talented, but so young. Yet, Alex was already working with me, and I was in the process of convincing Alison, who was languishing at Nike with her new MBA but little chance to use her skills, that she would have greater decision-making responsibility working at the winery. Her tradeoff would be a cut in pay. "I'll be bringing down the average salary of my MBA class," she grumbled, as she recounted how many of her friends had taken high paying jobs after graduation. I maintained hers shouldn't be a financial decision. "Don't let the lure of money sidetrack you," I told her. "This is about adventure and the thrill of learning to run your own business."

In the back of my mind, I had some doubts about our working together. It was clear to me that my smart, opinionated daughter was executive material. Armed with more MBA skills than I would ever have, she was poised and coolheaded. Yet she reminded me of my mother with her judgmental approach, always ready to appraise my actions. I didn't need a substitute for my mother, particularly my own daughter. I also had not yet completely recovered from her teenage years, when she'd had such disdain for me, a situation I considered payback for my teenage behavior.

I wasn't sure I wanted to be in the position of being her boss. I had railed against my mother telling me what to do; I could never have accepted her as my supervisor. Alison and I met with a counselor to discuss whether we could work together. We agreed to try. Alex, who had become a key part of the winery team, weighed in on our decision. "Dude," he said to Alison in his best big brother voice, "Are you willing for this to be the last job you ever have?" His solemn look made it was clear this was a serious question, one that indicated his own expectations. The idea that coming into the family business would last a lifetime might be normal practice in Europe, but unusual in the United States where people routinely moved from one job to another. Torn between a desire to make money and a desire to use her skills, Alison had thought hard before deciding. "Yes," she told him, her eyes bright with hope and enthusiasm.

Working with two of my children rekindled my energy; I looked forward to sharing what I knew about the wine business. If I were going to have protégés, I couldn't think of anyone better than my own progeny. With Alison's decision, I wanted to get going right away. We were creating a real family business now. I called Pat Frishkoff who had founded the Family Business Program at Oregon State University, to advise us on integrating another family member into the business. She came to meet with the three of us at my home in October, 2004, for what turned out to be the beginning of a three-year transition.

Growing up, I watched the 1950s TV show "What's My Line," in which a panel of celebrities tried to guess the occupation of the contestant, usually proving how deceiving appearances could be. Pat would have been an ideal player. She appeared to be a genial, frumpy homemaker until she started talking. Then the hard-nosed business expert with a laser-quick mind emerged.

On that brisk October day, Pat ambled into my living room, plunked down on the sofa, looked sharply at me, and zeroed in with her first question. "What will Mom do?" she asked bluntly, placing the focus of the transition squarely on me. I had no idea what I was going to do and the question made me recoil. Weren't we here to talk about Alex and Alison? But I had to say something. "I wrote a book that the University of California Press wants to publish. I guess I'll be promoting it," I stammered in response. With that explanation, Pat nodded. "If the kids are going to take over, we need to get Mom out of the way," she explained. I laughed with relief.

It would be years before I understood why Pat had started with me. The transitioning person needs to have something to look forward to, but I found the question presented a conundrum. What to do was the wrong question for me; I couldn't plan for the future until I had let go. Letting go turned out to be my first priority.

The four of us spent the afternoon creating new job descriptions for Alex and Alison and planning how to announce the addition of another family member to the staff. Alison began her new career, her "last job," in mid-November, 2004, as Director of Marketing. We didn't yet have a long-range plan. Alex and Alison had become my exit strategy, but I felt no threat to my position. Surrendering control was, at this point, a theoretical, cerebral concept. I could imagine them in the very vague future waiting for their chance, eager to take my place. But now they were still young pups.

They had a steep learning curve ahead of them, and they knew it. Running a vineyard and winery, despite its aura of glamour, was hard work, an all consuming, high-stakes enterprise. Our whole family depended on its success. I wanted Alex and Alison to experience the weight of the business. To accomplish that, I needed to give them enough responsibility so they would feel, all the way to their core, that the business rested on their shoulders.

During 2005, the whole next year, they each took pieces of my work and expanded the scope, Alex on sales and Alison on marketing. To see the big picture, I tried to include them in everything I did. They took in their new experiences with gusto, showing up for work each day with smiles, ready for the next challenge. I loved their spirit. Although premature, the big question in the back of their minds was who would be President. Both wanted it. When the time came, I would have to make a recommendation, and our family board would choose. I tried not to think about that.

Alex was older and had been with the winery longer. He starred as a people person, a natural salesman, compassionate, and creative. As the second son, he distinguished himself from Nik, his Stanford grad older brother, first with his quirky sense of humor and imagination, and later as a successful bicycle racer. His ability to connect with people had surfaced at an early age. When Grandma Betty, Bill's mother, came to see us, she always asked each of the kids about themselves. When he was five, Alex turned it around. "How was your day, Grandma?" Alex's warmth and charisma made him a presence in a room. I admired his easy banter, watching him engage people with a charm that was authentic and natural, and remarks that ranged from amusing to hilarious. On the other hand, his impulsiveness gave him a history of what I called "ready, fire, aim." In his enthusiasm, he took on more than he could handle, routinely double booking himself. I worried what he might let fall through the cracks.

Alison, like me, was more introverted. Tall, slim, and pretty, her drive and ambition weren't immediately obvious. She possessed a flair for organizing that surfaced in toddlerhood when she kept her toys sorted into brown shopping bags. As an adult, her color-coded calendar displayed her outstanding time management. After interning at a Portland public relations firm known for creative marketing, she worked at Nordstrom, where she learned first-rate customer service. Fluent with spreadsheets, she would be a well-organized and strategic administrator. But her fire flamed under a cool exterior, and her knack for taking command often veered toward the authoritarian.

I had my senior staff take the Meyers-Briggs personality tests and burst out laughing when Alex and Alison showed me their results. My two children were exact opposites on every score. I cringed at the thought of having to choose between them. The problem with having to select one was each had different strengths and was capable. I could imagine only unpleasant scenarios caused by the repercussions of choosing between siblings. This was far more emotionally charged than choosing between two unrelated employees. Pat could see that we were getting hung up with this dilemma.

"Stop talking about it and let it ride," she said. "Concentrate on the business at hand."

She had enough clout that we let the subject drop.

During the remainder of 2005 the board watched to see who would emerge as the obvious choice. Neither did. In January, 2006, when the family board met at Alison's house to make the final decision, Pat joined us. Alison and Alex had come up with a proposal which Alex announced.

"Alison will be the next President and I will be her Executive Vice President." Nik, Bill, and I sat stunned. I had thought Alex wanted it as much as Alison. I wondered what made him retreat and watched as Nik and Bill responded.

"Are you backing down to avoid a family fight?" Nik asked. "How did you arrive at this solution?"

Bill chimed in next, before Alex had a chance to answer. "Alex, don't submerge yourself to avoid controversy. That won't work in the long run."

Alison stayed silent as Alex straightened up in his chair with a determined look. "I admit the indecision wore me down," he said. I know either of us could be President. But only one of us would make a good Executive Vice President. Alison couldn't accept it, but I could. So I'm willing to do it." Alison looked sheepish and a moment of uncomfortable silence ensued. Pat, who had been watching our interaction, looked around.

"You don't have to choose," she said. "What's wrong with having co-presidents? It's unusual. It's not easy. But it's been done successfully. You have many advantages if you can share the leadership." She turned to Alison and asked her to consider what she would do if she were President, then became pregnant and wanted to take some time off to be with her new baby.

"If you and Alex shared the leadership," Pat continued, "and were essentially interchangeable, that would be possible."

"I hadn't thought of that," Alison responded, with a pensive look that said Pat's comment had hit home, although she had no way of knowing how prophetic Pat's comment would be. Alison had no children. Early in her marriage, she had announced that she didn't want to have kids. Her brothers couldn't believe she was serious. She had teased them, saying that after seeing how much trouble their kids were, she decided she didn't want any. But later, when the time came for her to start running the winery, she was four months pregnant.

Pat looked at Alex, "If there's shared leadership, not only do you have someone to talk to at your level, but you have the possibility of a life outside the winery." The muscles in Alex's face relaxed and his dimples reappeared as Pat's words sunk in. With a co-presidency, he would have more time with his twin boys, teaching them to throw a baseball, ride bikes, go backpacking. "That might work," he admitted. Bill, Nik, and I looked at each other. Our board hadn't seriously considered a co-presidency, but we knew that together they could be stronger than either one would be alone. We had often remarked that if we could fuse them into one, they would be an incredible force.

"Okay," said Alex, with the twinkly smile we knew meant something lighthearted was coming. "I'll agree if Alison promises to share the secret stash of gummy bears she keeps in her desk drawer; the one she thinks no one knows about."

"Well, I'll agree too if Alex promises to replenish the ones he's already taken from it," Alison quickly rejoined.

"I'll be around to keep you both in line," Nik finished, wielding his stern, older brother voice.

When the laughter stopped, we continued discussing the risks of a co-presidency and, after looking at it every which way, agreed it would be the best solution. The challenge was how to insure success with this unusual leadership plan. One safety net was to get them started with a business coach of their own. Our financial advisor, Jack, had been urging me to hire the woman who had helped him and his company. I had put off spending the money, but now it was time. We gave Marsia, their new coach, the charge of molding brother and sister into a dynamic duo, getting the future co-presidents in the habit of respecting and communicating with each other, discussing issues rationally, and dealing with disagreement before something big arose.

The family had cleared a major hurdle with an elegant solution. I couldn't help being envious. The old saying about being lonely at the top was true. I often wished I had a peer to share the inner workings of the business. I was always aware of my singular position. As the employer, I had to be careful how much I confided in the people I hired. At any time, they could leave and take my confidences with them.

I had decided to start the transition process in the fall of 2004. It had taken a little over a year to settle the presidential dilemma. Alex and Alison could now look forward to running the winery and vineyard together. Over the first half of 2006, they met often with their new coach, working to articulate their vision for the business and create a plan for the final piece of the transition. They crafted a page of promises made to each other about communicating and dealing with issues. I stayed out of the process. My time was filled with the day-to-day problems of running the winery as well as my book's publication.

The device that would "get Mom out of the way" finally appeared in May, 2006. I paged through my advance copy of ***At Home in the Vineyard***, full of wonder at seeing my adult life spilled out in print. When I had started, more than five years earlier, I wrote by categories, dividing the story by family, neighbors, pets, farming, and so forth. Copious pages of writing, totally disconnected, stared back at me. I couldn't decide how to tie it all together. When I finally decided to tell it chronologically, as I had experienced it, Alex gave me this pointer: "Mom," he said, "why don't you organize it by the different hair styles you've had? Remember how long your hair was when you worked in the vineyard? You had braids. That was your Mother Earth phase. You cut your hair shorter when you ran for office to look more business-like. When you took over the winery, you turned blonde and stylish. After you were President for a while, you became silver and distinguished." I laughed. But he was spot on. My hair said it all; history by hairdo.

Writing helped me understand and come to terms with my vineyard and winery life. By articulating how working in the vineyard had tied me to the land, giving me a sense of place, and how learning to run the business had given me a confidence I'd never had, I could trace the evolution of my adulthood and my public persona. Used to looking forward and focusing on the next challenge, seeing my published book gave me a rare feeling of accomplishment.

6

2006

With the appearance of my book, I became a published author. It was a major achievement. Simultaneously moving back to the vineyard, returning to the place I felt I belonged, marked another. Bill and I had built a house on our vineyard in 1973 when I was pregnant with Alex. We lived there almost twenty years. Then, in the early 1990s, after I became President of the winery and Bill returned to work in Portland, we decided that since three of the four of us spent the day in Portland, it made sense to live there and sell the vineyard house. Nik was in college at the time, but Alex and Alison were in school in Portland. I didn't mind the fifty-minute commute back to the winery. Portland offered great restaurants, theater, and shopping which were a treat after being in the country for twenty years. When I left Bill, I stayed in Portland. My emotions were too raw to go back to the vineyard. There was no house to move back to anyway. I continued to commute to the winery.

When Russ and I decided to live together, in 1999, we bought a house in a suburban community, twenty minutes from the winery and half an hour from Portland. We thought being in-between would be perfect, but soon changed our minds. Summer dinners on our deck were invariably accompanied by the smell of our neighbor's dryer sheets. We were sure she waited until we came outside to sit on our deck for dinner before loading up her dryer with perfumed dryer sheets and turning it on. Weekends the power tools came out: lawn mowers, leaf blowers, pressure washers. Up and down the street, from sunup to sundown, a cacophony of lawn grooming and driveway washing filled the air.

I missed the quiet beauty of the vineyard and realized I was ready to go back. If we moved to the vineyard, we'd have to build. When Russ considered what a hassle that would be, he balked. When he saw how much it meant to me, he acquiesced. We negotiated with each other and with Alex and Alison for months over where on the property to build. Russ envisioned a home with a view on top of the hill, but it was unthinkable to use a prime grape site for a house. Alex suggested we consider building at the base of the vineyard where the winery had an old mobile home, acquired in the 1970s as part of a land purchase for vineyards. It was 100 yards from his house.

"Do you really want us living so close to you?" I asked.

"Sure, Mom. It's a great replacement for the mobile home." He didn't need to mention how handy it would be to have Grandma next door as a potential babysitter. The site with the mobile home was flat and uninteresting. It bordered the busy winery road where a row of seventy-five foot evergreen trees (for which Bill and I had bartered wine and planted as six foot saplings in the 1970s) shielded the area from winery traffic. Russ wanted water and could envision landscaping a little creek leading to a small pond. When I agreed to a pond with koi, Russ agreed to build in the spot I wanted. Two years into the business transition, in June of 2006, we moved to the vineyard. It was all new to Russ, but I had come home.

That summer, after six months spent formulating their vision for the winery, Alex and Alison unveiled their formal Transition Plan to the family board. With confidence and authority, they looked squarely at their father, mother, and older brother and presented an elaborate document, evidence of significant thought and work. They explained the promises they had made to each other about how they would work together; presented a timeline with milestone dates for transfer of power and new hires; listed job descriptions and staffing flow charts for now and future expansion. Expansion! The first thing they wanted to do was expand? Bill, Nik, and I were a little startled to see these "youngsters" firmly at the helm and ready to grow.

The plan had the future co-presidents slowly taking over my areas of responsibility during the remaining five months of 2006, then running daily operations for a year under my oversight, their "practice" year. I would remain President until January 2008, when the formal hand-off would occur. We approved the plan, and our "intentional transition," as it we learned it was called in family business lingo, now had an official document to guide us.

I had been told early on how rare it was for a family to prepare for a generational transition. That didn't make sense to me. Why wouldn't a family business want to plan for the future? By the end of our transition, I understood. From the time I first spoke with Pat, she repeatedly told me how critical I was to the process and how easily I could sabotage it.

I needed to be careful not to back away too fast, but also not to make decisions that Alex and Alison should be making. Being overly critical would be harmful, as would getting in between Alex and Alison when they clashed, rather than letting them work out their differences.

"Blatant acts of holding on aren't the danger," Pat said. "We can easily identify and deal with those. It's the unintentional acts of interfering that will cripple the process." It struck me as curious that I could impose the same deleterious effect on the transition regardless of whether I acted out of spite or love. I remembered one of my mother's favorite sayings: "The road to hell is paved with good intentions." It subsequently ran as a loop in the back of my mind, reminding me that the transition's success rested on me. From then on, with every move, I questioned whether I was doing the right thing.

Except for Russ, none of my employees knew yet that I would be stepping back. We were waiting for the final plan. Pat had warned me to consider how the staff would react since their allegiance was to me. The first challenge for the co-presidents-in-training would be to gain respect. My kids would have to learn to manage a staff that was older than they were. I would have to give them the freedom to do it.

I announced the new leadership to the six members of our senior staff at our 2006 fall retreat. "I need your help," I told our key employees, all of whom I had hired, as we sat around a large table in a conference room at a Portland hotel. "We need to work together to pass on to the next generation all the knowledge we have accumulated."

My announcement immediately gave Alex and Alison new status. When the senior staff responded by looking to them, the transition took a sudden turn. For the first time, I felt in my gut the future reality that they would be the leaders, not I. Until that moment, the idea of surrendering control had been purely intellectual. The discomfort of that moment, as I realized what I was giving up, was my first glimpse that the path ahead might be more gut wrenching than anticipated. Indeed, more than a year of emotional chaos lay ahead.

One Sunday morning, at the end of December 2006, I sat at my desk at home, glumly contemplating the official-looking papers staring back at me. Signing them would change my world. Before year's end, I needed to give away ownership of what I had built my life around. My attorney had told me that it wasn't good estate planning for me to own controlling shares of the family business. The winery had become so valuable that, if something should happen to me, the estate taxes would cripple the business. An easy solution existed. As part of the transition, I should gift enough shares of stock to my three children to break my control.

But what seemed so simple on paper didn't account for human emotions. There was a stumbling block. Me. It had taken me years to become the majority owner. I liked the feeling of ownership control. I had put so much of myself into building the business that it was a child I didn't want to lose, even though it had grown to the point that I knew I needed to let it go. The papers before me unleashed strong forces squabbling ferociously between my ears. The argument needed to be settled. Red plastic arrows pointed to the signature lines on the crisp new stock certificates to gift to Nik, Alex, and Alison, enough shares to break my ownership control of Sokol Blosser Winery. It had been exactly thirty-six years since Bill and I had started our vineyard.

Outside my window, the somber winter scene reflected my mood. Rows of bare grapevines advanced in stoic silence up the hill-side, a still-life army marching in formation, impervious to the chill wind sweeping past. Only the tiny house finches, flitting among the dead seed heads along the stream, showed any life. I glanced back at my desk, hoping that the papers had magically disappeared. No, they were still there, waiting for me. This was something I couldn't delegate. I had come into my little office to confront this piece of the transition that I'd been putting off. Russ was still at the breakfast table engrossed in the paper. The cat took one look outside and curled up next to him. The house had settled into its Sunday morning stillness. The only noise was inside my head. I stared silently at the certificates, while the battle played out and a winner declared. I watched myself pick up the pen and saw my hand start signing, methodically eliminating the red tabs.

With hindsight, I see there were really three voices involved: a rational business voice looking out for the interests of the winery; a quiet inner voice intuitively sensing what was best for the family; and an intensely emotional ego which spoke up to protect its public persona. In the end, the first two banded together to barely defeat the powerful third. After signing, I would still carry the title of President during one more year of transition, but I was no longer the majority owner. My era had legally ended.

Since that day, the anguish of picking up the pen and voluntarily signing away what I had worked so hard, and given up so much to get, has faded. At the time, I found myself left with two consequential issues for the future. When I was no longer President, what would happen to the business? Then, more personally and equally important, what would happen to me? I had answers to neither.

For years I had watched the relentless flow of life in the vineyard, one season ebbing into the next. It was the cycle of life, arising and dissolving over and over. The vineyard always renewed itself. I hoped I would too.

7

2007

To describe the final year of the transition simply as arduous or challenging doesn't do justice to the complex, puzzling, awkward, and emotional roller coaster ride that 2007 became. Dubbed the "practice year," I was to be President in name only. Alex and Alison would take over all daily operations. This left me in a quandary: I wanted them to take the reins and make decisions, but as titular President, I was responsible. What if I thought they were making a mistake?

It was hard not to tell them what to do, especially when they hesitated over easy decisions, so it didn't take me long to stumble. I seesawed from total withdrawal to taking over. Alex and Alison never knew which way I would go, but then, neither did I. I had envisioned my children coming to me with situations that I, as the wise elder, would ask key questions to help them work through. It never got further than being a sweet dream. I was no Socrates.

Alex proposed an Executive Committee of the key managers, with the idea of making decisions by consensus. I went along, willing to try Alex's approach, although my mode of operation had been to make decisions alone, often asking for input first. The five of us would meet weekly at a set time and he would lead the meetings. We implemented his plan, nicknaming it X-Com.

At the first meeting, the others came into the office Alex and I shared and took seats around the small table. Alex explained that on X-Com we would discuss issues, so each department knew what the others were doing, and make administrative decisions together. I smiled my assent when the others looked to me. We then went around the table, each person reporting on what they were doing and bringing up issues for discussion and decisions. I intended to let the others make policy decisions but, following precedent, they soon turned to me for advice. I wish I could say I smiled sagely and asked what they would suggest doing, but that didn't happen. Before I could stop myself, I gave advice, like I was used to doing. Then, when I stopped to take a breath, I realized I'd broken my resolve not to intervene. My mother's refrain about the road to hell rang loudly in my ears.

That was just the start. Alex didn't show his frustration, but if I were him, I would have been livid. The trouble was that I had seen most of the problems before and knew what needed to be done. I intended to transfer an educated, intuitive ability to make decisions to those who didn't have my experience, but my exasperation and impatience at the fumbling usually triumphed. We had endless discussions, for example, about whether we should move to colorful printed cases for our wines or continue to follow our custom of simply putting a wine label on the case to identify it. There were countervailing arguments for each alternative from marketing, financial, and environmental angles. The committee couldn't decide what to do. With no resolution in sight, impatience trumped my resolve. My speaking up hijacked the meeting, ending the discussion without giving the team the chance to work it out themselves. A wide piece of duct tape over my mouth might have helped, although I'm pretty sure I could have talked through it.

One morning, Alex came into our joint office, grinning like a cat that had just caught a mouse. He sat down and looked at me earnestly with his dimpled smile.

"Mom, I thought of what your new title should be." I hadn't been thinking ahead to what my title would be when it was no longer President, but clearly Alex and Alison had. I looked at him inquisitively.

"Founder!" he said enthusiastically. Indicative of my state of mind, my immediate reaction was cynical and negative. Perfect, I thought – vague and meaningless, but important-sounding. I didn't say that to him. It was a sweet gesture on his part.

"Good thinking, Alex," I lied. "Founder sounds fine. Thank you."

Alison had followed him in.

"Mom, we want you to write your new job description," she said. "Tell us what you want to do."

Another sweet gesture that only provoked gloom. I interpreted the question as asking what relatively unimportant activity I would be satisfied doing.

With no idea how to approach writing my job description, I called Pat for advice. She responded she'd be interested in what I came up with. "Since transferring control is rare, you're charting new ground," she told me. "Family businesses don't usually address this. The retiring founder just does whatever he or she wants." That sounded fine for the founder but what about the good of the business? If the parents or founder didn't plan for the future, the business headed towards chaos. Yet, a job description presented a challenge. Here was a position no company would hire. This situation would surface only in a family business when a parent who had built and run the company wanted to stay on in some capacity while the kids took the reins. I wondered if I was trying to do the impossible by giving up control and sticking around. Perhaps my years as president and my penchant for decision-making would prevent me from taking any other role. If I had known exactly what I wanted to do as Founder, it would have helped, but since I couldn't envision myself in any role other than President, I was clueless how to proceed.

I wondered if I could find a role as mentor, cheerleader, or keeper of the vision; something that would be an asset to the company and not just a drag on the payroll. With that goal in mind, I crafted a list of possibilities and sent it off to Pat to get her opinion. With characteristic bluntness, she wrote back, using words like "vague," "meddling," "second-guess." Apparently, my job description had omitted some important items. "Who would you report to?" she asked. "Who decides where you would travel, what events you would participate in, and what community programs you would support?" Whoa! I could feel my heart pound at the thought of having to ask my children for permission to do some peripheral thing in the business I had built, controlled, and dominated over twenty years. Alex and Alison would listen to my requests, but when I stepped back they would be the decision makers, not me.

Pat asked if my being the cheerleader for the staff would make Alex and Alison be the bad cops. She pointed out that here was a way I could unintentionally sabotage my kids. My stomach knotted up reading her comments. Here I was, with the best of intentions, falling into the trap I was trying so hard to avoid. I didn't want to go back, but I was having trouble going forward. I hadn't thought about watching Alex and Alison make decisions that I didn't agree with, or going to them for approval of my activities. That would be tough. Yet, it was clear that I needed to stand back, to let them take charge.

I didn't want to dampen Alex and Alison's enthusiasm, but I didn't know how to shut up. Don't complain; be supportive, I kept telling myself. Sometimes I wondered if I could do it. I was not turning out to be the upbeat, cheerful, encouraging person I had envisioned. Every time I saw a staff member go to Alex or Alison for advice instead of coming to me, a physical pang shot through me, even though that was what needed to happen. Bill told me later he doubted all during the transition whether I would be able to go through with it. My family saw clearly the little cloud of gloom that floated above me.

The powerlessness of my new role had hit home and it baffled me. I wasn't sure if it was the loss of control that roiled my gut or no longer being important or useful. Alex and Alison needed to feel responsibility for the business at the gut level, and the only way to achieve that was to give them full control. I needed to step back. I wanted to step back. But every time I tried, I faltered. I couldn't understand why this was so hard.

Early in the year I had seen a Buddhist quote in the newspaper, which caught my attention. "In the end, only three things matter: how fully you have lived, how deeply you have loved, and how well you have learned to let go." The last phrase flashed in neon colors. Everybody knows the first two – it's what life is about. Self-help books are full of advice on learning to live to the fullest, embracing opportunity, learning to love.

The buzz is about getting more, which is what I'd done all my life, striving to accumulate knowledge, experience, expertise, influence, material well being. Business is all about growth and expansion. Cutting back denoted failure or weakness. Deciding to give up my winery presidency may have felt right, but it went against everything I had been trained to do. I knew how to aspire to get ahead, not how to let go. 2007 taught me that transitioning out of my role as President demanded the same sort of courage and willpower that had helped me move forward. The energy just had to be focused differently. I had learned on the job to be President. Now I had to learn NOT to be President the same painful way.

One morning it started snowing and Alex and Alison decided to close the tasting room. I didn't know about it until Alison emailed everyone announcing their decision. A torrent of protest rose up inside me: They can't do that! They have to keep the tasting room open. What if someone drove all the way through the snow and found it closed? That would be such bad public relations. I would have kept it open for even a few customers rather than disappoint anyone. They should have asked me beforehand. Should I tell them this is a mistake?

Then, in the middle of my outrage, something occurred to me. Wait, they're in charge; this is their decision to make. Even though I think it's the wrong one, I have to let them make the decisions and face the consequences. Chastising them could sabotage the transition. Remember, the road to hell is paved with good intentions.

Maybe I was being overly critical. My emotions were running so high, I'd lost perspective and wanted to scream with frustration. The only thing I could think of to calm me down was to bundle up and walk in the vineyard. By early afternoon, the sun had started to melt the snow, leaving puddles and wet mud. My boots sloshed noisily as I walked from our house slowly up to the winery. I grimaced at the Closed sign on the tasting room, and continued up the hill, past an area being readied for spring replanting. The old vines which had been removed formed a giant pile in the middle of the muddy field, waiting to be burned. I trudged on, to the edge of the highest part of the vineyard, bordered by a wooded canyon and stood still, taking it all in. Only the melting ice dripping off the tall firs broke the silence. In the healing quiet of the snowy vineyard, my anger started to soften.

I walked back down the hill, passing the spot where the giant bigleaf maple used to harbor grape-eating birds. During harvest, swarms of migrating birds would sit in the tree and mock us. We finally gave in and chopped the tree down, hiring someone to come with a giant machine to grind out the stump. I walked through another part of the vineyard that used to be filled with Brooks prune trees. When I ran the vineyard, I'd circle them on the tractor, pulling the cultivator, ducking under branches to get close to the tree trunk. I remembered where I found the first of many little goldfinch nests. Nostalgia for past farming days welled up in me, although they were tough times and looked better only in hindsight. Back home an hour later, my anger was spent. The vineyard had worked its magic. I never said a word to Alex or Alison about it.

Alison suggested perhaps my working with their business coach would be worth trying. At first I declined. I was strong enough to do this alone, wasn't I? I had no mentors I could turn to and wasn't used to asking for help. But when I asked the question, I faced the answer and relented.

To my surprise, having a neutral person with whom I could talk openly gave me tremendous relief. Embarrassed and confused by my feelings, I found comfort talking to someone who neither condemned nor ridiculed, but listened and assured me that what I was undergoing was normal.

Alex and Alison had taken over finance and production, the last domains under my control as the practice year began. Alison started supervising the accounting office and Alex took over the winery and the vineyard. I knew the biggest challenge would be in the winery, with Alex supervising Russ. Because we worked so well together, Russ didn't want that synergy to end. He did not look forward to my leaving. As a hands-on winemaker, controlling every aspect of the winemaking process, he worried that under Alex and Alison's plans for expansion, he would lose that ability. If production got too large, it would be more than he could handle. He had also reservations about working for Alex, since Russ's attention to detail and Alex's easygoing style didn't mesh.

Russ, like me, had also been a sole decision maker. He didn't want to share winemaking responsibility. Seeing Russ accept Alex meant a lot to me. I loved and understood them both and kept trying to explain Alex to Russ and Russ to Alex. Alex finally put a halt to my meddling. "Mom," he said. "Please stop triangulating. If Russ has a problem, tell him to come to me." It felt odd to have my son scold me, but I had to admit he was right. The next time Russ complained to me about something Alex had done, or not done, I told him to talk to Alex about it. Once I got out of the way, they learned to work together.

Alex moved more easily into managing the vineyard, and giving up that arena was the most emotionally conflicted piece for me. Managing the vineyard in the 1980s had connected me to the land with a new emotional force. I had been a suburban girl whose childhood view of nature was flower borders decorating spacious lawns or lush grass on a golf course. Before the vineyard I'd never grown anything more than a sweet potato, held with toothpicks in a glass of water. But living next to the vines, I experienced the rhythm of the changing seasons and the beauty of the vineyard cycle. Appreciation of nature seeped in over twenty years, leaving me with a profound respect for the earth and a sense of the interconnection of all things, living and nonliving – all part of a gigantic whole.

In the last decade of my presidency I had taken the vineyard organic, motivated by concern for the environment and the pollution caused by agricultural chemicals. By the time Congress passed national organic standards in 2000, I had fully embraced the paradigm of farming that emphasized healthy soil in which microbial life supplied nutrients to plants and held the soil in place. Conventional farming didn't give such prominence to the soil, relying on chemicals that fed the plant but killed the microbes which kept the soil healthy. While I was deciding whether to go through the mountain of paperwork that organic certification entailed, I joined a group of colleagues who were studying biodynamics, another farming approach coming into vogue. We hired a biodynamic horticulturist to come up from California once a month to instruct us.

We started by studying the founder of biodynamics, an early twentieth century Austrian named Rudolf Steiner, whose vision was to revitalize the earth by connecting natural science and mysticism. Steiner took organic principles to a paranormal level, invoking not only the cosmos, but also otherworld dimensions. Organic farming operated on the assumption that the earth was a complex biological system. Biodynamics envisioned the earth as part of a living cosmos, dependent on planetary movement. Was Steiner a nut or had he hit on something? Our instructor talked at length about invisible energetic forces that converted non-matter into matter inside the vine. He told us that biodynamic preparations enlivened the soil like yeast enlivens dough.

We had come together to find practical farming solutions, not indulge in mystical theory. We wanted to protect our vines from disease and destructive insects. Most of us had enough trouble coordinating labor, weather, and equipment readiness to accomplish farming procedures. Taking into account the phase of the moon and the stations of the planets for each procedure was a stretch.

Our instructor emphasized the importance of spraying plant essences during the growing season, such as chamomile flowers, dandelion leaves, yarrow, nettle, and valerian. "Don't drench the vines like with other sprays, just aim a gentle mist into the air, and let the energy float down onto the vines." You had to be a believer to go to all that trouble. Plant essences were not available in the chemical aisles at our local farm stores. We had to plan ahead and mail order them. But there was a reason we went to the trouble of learning something so difficult to understand and so foreign to our thinking. What got our attention was that the best vineyards in France, the Mother Lode of wine, had embraced biodynamics.

For two years, in 2002 and 2003, I experimented, setting aside two vineyard blocks to farm biodynamically. This took ignoring Luis's, my vineyard manager, and Alex's incredulity. I procured the plant essence sprays, and then had to follow the proper application ritual. I asked Luis to have his crew lash together pruned grape canes to make a stick broom, on which any black garbed witch would have been proud to fly. This creation was then used to stir the spray formulations, going in alternating directions to create a vortex, for thirty to sixty minutes, depending on the spray. I also had them construct a compost pile, with grape pomace, cow manure, and straw. It looked like a giant, thirty foot long, six-foot high lasagna, which I then inoculated with special biodynamic preparations. Luis did it all without complaining, although I imagined he rolled his eyes behind my back and used choice words explaining these unusual procedures to his crew.

The second year of our experimentation, I hired Philippe, a French biodynamic viticulturist who consulted for me once a month. On one spring visit, as the vineyard glistened in the cool morning air, Alex and Luis accompanied Philippe and me as we walked through our biodynamic blocks. The new grape shoots, with their tiny green leaves and miniature clusters, shimmered with morning dew. Eager to learn, I felt like a puppy scampering through the vineyard, trying to keep up with my lanky consultant. Philippe stopped periodically to stare intently at the vines, the three of us halting in our tracks behind him. He barked a command for my next vineyard procedure. What was he seeing? What did the vine look like through a biodynamic lens? I asked. Philippe peered down at me with that condescending look the French are so good at. "I'm looking," he said, with splendid pomposity, "at the quality of light," and strode on down the row.

As we continued, stepping over gopher mounds on our walk, I asked what he recommended we do about the gophers that were creating havoc in the vineyard. He told us to catch some, cut off their heads, and put them on stakes around the vineyard. I'll never forget the look Alex and Luis gave each other. That was the last season Philippe consulted for us.

When Alex took over the vineyards as part of the transition, he chose to concentrate on organic farming rather than biodynamic.

He'd had it with vineyard consultants. "Mom," he said, "our years on this land and our understanding of our vines are worth more than the crackpots who have come in and given us bad advice. Our common sense is better than their so-called expertise. Just because they call themselves experts doesn't mean they are."

I understood his decision and agreed with his view of consultants, but connecting spirituality with farming fascinated me. By seeing the farm as a living cosmic system, every part intertwined, from the planets, to the farmer, down to the microbes and rocks in the soil, biodynamics expanded my understanding of universal interdependence – as well as introduced the idea of cosmic energy flow, a theme I would keep running into.

When I turned responsibility for the vineyard over to Alex at the start of 2007, I gave him my trusty old Radio Shack weather band radio as the token of his ultimate responsibility for vineyard decisions, so many of which are based on weather. I was glad he loved the vineyard as I did and took his new responsibility with great seriousness, but another physical pang hit me as Alex became the decision-maker. The vineyard harbored an important part of my psyche. I told Marsia that turning the vineyards over to Alex was the right thing to do, but it made me so sad.

"I've got a word for you," she said. "Grief."

I associated grief with death. Nobody was dying. I was almost three years into the transition process before realizing that grief was part of the process of letting go. I was giving up something that defined me – letting a part of me die. I remembered the line from *The Fantasticks* that had grabbed my attention when I first heard it: "You have to die a bit before you grow again." Now I understood what it meant. Grief may have been a normal reaction, but it came as a surprise. I hadn't anticipated feeling so sorrowful. Suddenly whole days went by where nothing sounded interesting or worth doing. Work deadlines kept me from staring aimlessly into space. I wondered how many more unforeseen emotional jolts were lying in wait.

Marsia gave me a homework assignment she said would help bring closure to the past and allow me to move forward. She told me to think about the business and write answers to the following: What was I disappointed about? What did I regret? What did I resent? What was I pleased about? What had I accomplished? Who would I like to acknowledge for their help? What would I like to be acknowledged for?

As she rattled off these questions, my mind immediately went blank. When I told her I couldn't think of what to say, she started interrogating. Wasn't I pleased with how well our Evolution label was doing? Wasn't I pleased to have hired Russ? Wasn't I pleased that the business was in good shape and ready to turn over to the kids to launch to the next level? Didn't I have decisions I regretted and people – employees, suppliers, and customers – that I longed to tell off? Didn't I have regrets about some of the people I'd hired? Did I have any tensions left around Bill and the business? How about the industry as a whole? The stuck couplings in my brain started to click open, although I wasn't quite ready to start writing. I let her questions percolate.

In February 2007, Alison and I flew to Chicago to appear at a conference for family businesses. We had been asked to participate in a panel discussion sponsored by the Family Business Center at Loyola University. The topic was transition: how family businesses pass on their ethics, values, responsibility, and power. I felt honored to have been invited but embarrassed to be considered an expert when I felt so incompetent handling my situation. All I could do was to speak frankly about what a hard time I was having.

We shared the panel with another family. Listening to them, two brothers who were fourth generation in their family business, it became apparent that once a family business passes to succeeding generations, it can take on a life of its own. In the best cases, transitions are planned. The brothers had known they would take over the business and had been groomed for it. They talked about how they saw themselves as temporary custodians of the business. This was a significantly different mindset from mine. As a first generation founder, I regarded the business as personal property. I was in the process of learning what it meant to pass the business to the next generation.

After our panel, we mingled with the conference attendees. Their comments helped me understand how unusual our "intentional transition" at Sokol Blosser was, especially for a first generation business. One man told me that the first time he knew he would be President of his family's business was when his father announced the news at their company Christmas party. The son had been humiliated rather than thrilled; he wished to be involved in the decision, like a partner. Instead he felt treated like a child. I understood his anguish but also the father's thinking. The father looked at the business as his to give and probably thought the surprise announcement would be a wonderful present. I imagine the father anticipated bestowing the presidency on his son with pleasure and was surprised and hurt by the son's reaction.

People came up to tell me they wished their parents would face their exit instead of continuing on with no planning. One woman said her parents talked vaguely about retirement, and took more vacation time every year, but couldn't bring themselves to make plans for the future of the business. Doing nothing, the path of least resistance, seemed common. Look how hard it was for me – and I wanted to do it. What propelled me forward was my conviction that the welfare of the company hinged on my surrendering control. For Alex and Alison to feel the weight of the business, they had to be the decision makers.

Of course the key issue for parents, whose lives have been tied up in the business, was what to do next, so that question kept appearing. One man, who had been through the transition process, told me how much more balanced his life was. He engaged in a number of activities – some business, some nonprofit volunteering, some sports, some travel, some family time, with none of them dominating. I tucked away his advice to ponder later. I wasn't ready to think about the future. As President of the winery, all my emotional and intellectual energy was still tied up running it. I needed to pass the baton smoothly to the next generation, and all effort was going towards that goal. I had no idea what would come next and spent no time dreaming of future pursuits.

Instinctively, I sensed that letting go had to come first. I had to work at protecting that stance. "What are you going to do?" was everyone's first concern. If you're not doing this, what will you do, seemed the obvious question. I've since had successful people confess that they wish they could let go, but would need to know what they would do instead. They couldn't leave the comfort of the known, even if they didn't like it. Letting go as weakness? No way. The transition taught me that letting go tested courage, faith, and resilience.

Marsia's homework turned out to be cathartic. When I finally sat down to do it, the words poured across my computer screen, revealing how much I had harbored inside. I confessed regrets and disappointments kept suppressed because they seemed petty or didn't fit how I wanted to think of myself. Things I was still angry about surfaced, from small slights or criticism, to stupid moves I'd made. I had much forgiving to do, not the least of which was myself. What came up was private and personal and often painful – people I wished I hadn't hired; others I wished I'd treated better; anger at consultants who gave bad advice; frustration at decisions that didn't turn out as expected; snubs from wine writers and other winery owners that I took personally. By the time I stopped typing, a long list had emerged.

Then I wrote about the good things, what I had accomplished. I surprised myself with how far I had come. Armed only with history and teaching degrees, I had become a business executive. My daddy would be proud. If he were alive we could be talking business and sipping wine.

8

Transition Troubles

Part of what I had loved about running the winery was resolving situations with no right answers, requiring resourceful thinking. There was an unending supply of these over the years. Should we try to expand our export markets? If so, where? How big a discount could we offer our club members? Were brochures really an effective marketing tool? What kind of winery events would attract customers? How many cases of each wine should we make? Would hiring additional sales people pay for itself?

Transferring the problem-solving to Alex and Alison left me with just one ongoing challenge – letting go of that role. Facing difficult issues and keeping cool in a crisis had been my strengths. I thought they would help me make the transition. I was wrong. When I saw a problem, my drive to fix things trumped everything. Winter and spring of the "practice year," despite intending to be a wise elder, I ruefully concluded that meddling buttinsky would be a more fitting description.

I had no problem letting Alex and Alison negotiate purchasing another parcel of land to plant vines, and managing an office addition, as the board had close oversight of both. It was the everyday decisions in the areas of my special interest, especially vineyard management and marketing, that I couldn't stay out of. Walking through the vineyard one day, I noticed that the crew had done a sloppy job in one section of tying up the canes and the grape clusters looked squished together. This would be the perfect condition for rot to occur. I felt I should alert Alex. Maybe he needed to find out who had worked that section and have him go back and fix it. When I told Alex, I discovered that he already knew and had decided not to tell me. I couldn't understand why, when he knew how interested and involved I was with the vineyard, that he didn't consult or bother to keep me informed. I felt we might be dangerously close to total lack of communication.

We needed the safety of our consultant's office for Alex to admit he didn't feel comfortable sharing a problem with me because he knew I'd want to fix it. Alison said she wanted to figure out a solution for herself, not have me tell her. Their message was clear: I needed to give up what, to me, was one of the joys of running a business. No wonder I was grieving.

After one episode, when I realized I had overstepped, I felt so badly, I emailed Alex and Alison, apologizing for interfering and telling them I would try harder to stop solving their problems. I imagined them giving each other knowing looks with the same thought – mom would butt in again; it was just a question of when.

What a peculiar position. If Alex and Alison had suddenly decided they didn't want to go through with it and wanted me to be President again, I wouldn't be happy. I didn't want my old job back. But my feet felt stuck in clay as I tried to go forward. So many times I asked myself why. On a good day I could laugh at myself, trying to let go yet clinging at the same time.

One morning Alison came into my office, which I shared with Alex. We were in the process of adding office space, but I liked sharing with Alex. It was close but companionable, and we often got into productive spontaneous conversations. "Can we talk to you?" she asked. I gestured her to a seat. When she took it, Alex came over to stand behind her. They were up to something.

"Mom, we've been thinking," Alison began. She looked directly at me, her blue eyes wary but determined. Alex would have chatted a bit first, warming into it; Alison came right to the point. "Would you be willing to move out of your office so Alex and I could be together?"

My surprise at her unexpected request must have showed; she looked taken aback. My first thought was that while this may have sounded like a question, I really didn't have a choice. If I said no, I'd be sabotaging the transition. I didn't want to move, but I was stuck.

"We need to be able to talk to each other," she went on, with a calmness she couldn't have felt, "being in the same office would help a lot." Was this a coup d'état? A vision of myself dethroned, relegated to a tiny closet office, flashed through my mind. I could feel my face redden as I started to crumble inside. Tears welled up and I desperately hoped none would escape. I had come to work that morning thinking I was fine and couldn't understand such an emotional reaction.

The rational side of me understood their request. I tried to squash the emotion and keep tears at bay by taking a practical approach.

"Where do you want me to move?" I asked.

"There's an empty desk in the big sales room where you could work," Alex assured me, revealing they had thought this through. It took backbone for them to ask their mother, the President, to vacate the office she had used for sixteen years. I was so busy fighting back the lump in my throat and the high probability of tears, I didn't appreciate their courage until later. They probably didn't know how upset I was.

After blathering my consent, my computer and the contents of my desk were moved with amazing speed. Within thirty minutes, before I had time to protest, change my mind, or cry, I found myself sitting at a desk in an open office. The three others in the office smiled and welcomed me, then appeared hard at work. I sat and stared at my new desk, telling myself it was silly to feel humiliated. I should be looking at giving up my office as a generous gesture, but in my depressed state, I felt kicked out. I missed my privacy and the easy camaraderie with Alex. I did, however, have the feeling that my new office mates might be working harder than they did before I moved in next to them.

I was glad to leave on a long-anticipated sales trip to Atlanta and Toronto, taking Alison with me. We were going first to Atlanta for the High Museum Wine and Art Auction and then to Toronto for our importer's Chairman's Gala. The Atlanta auction was an event I had worked for many years, developing good friends and winery relationships. I wanted to introduce Alison, who would attend in the future. In Toronto, I had planned a winery dinner accompanied by a reading from ***At Home in the Vineyard***, my new book. Alison agreed to continue the trip with me. She didn't really see a role for herself in Toronto and told people "I'm going as mom's baggage handler."

After a successful few days in Atlanta, we headed for Toronto where we planned to visit an old friend whose family I had lived with in Japan. Sachiko, who was now living in Toronto to be with her son and his family, had planned a dinner party to celebrate my book. She'd even hired a Japanese chef to cook my favorite Japanese foods. Alison and I had arrived on Sunday at midday and saw Sachiko's table already set for ten, complete with name cards at each place, flowers, company china, and candles. The chef and his helper were in the kitchen; she had gone all out for this dinner.

Sachiko's family had hosted me in their home in Tokyo as an AFS exchange student in 1961, when I was sixteen. When, after three months, I returned home to Milwaukee, I was so enamored of Japan – the architecture, décor, customs, food – I talked about nothing else. My brothers rolled their eyes whenever I spoke of it. When I made them green tea, they said it tasted just like hot water. "I bet you couldn't tell the difference blindfolded," one said. "Can so," I said. "Let's see," another challenged. So I brewed a fresh pot of tea. They tied a handkerchief around my eyes and set three cups in front of me to taste. Two tasted like water, but the third had the rich taste of the green tea I loved. "This one's the tea," I exclaimed triumphantly. As I pulled off my blindfold, they were laughing so hard they couldn't talk. "They were all hot water!," one brother hooted, in between peals of laughter. Being the little sister was never easy.

I called Sachiko my Japanese sister and we had kept up with each other over the years. She was studying in the United States when I got married in 1966 and was able to be one of my bridesmaids. She visited Bill and me with her husband and baby boy when we were starting the vineyard, then later after a painful divorce, when her son was a college student in Washington State. I had gone back to Tokyo twice, once with Bill on a wine trip in the early 1980s and once alone, on my way back from an International Women's Forum conference in Singapore, in 2000. On the latter trip, I was able to visit the home where I had stayed so many years ago, shortly before it was torn down to make way for multiple unit housing. I told my Japanese brothers and sisters how sad it made me feel to see this beautiful traditional Japanese home and garden demolished. The oldest brother of the family, who still lived in the house, said, with no show of the emotion I know he felt, that the land it sat on was too valuable for a single family home.

At Sachiko's home in Toronto, coming down the stairs in my silk suit for the party, just before 5:00 PM, I slipped off the bottom step, unexpectedly more narrow than the others, rolled my right ankle and heard a crack as I landed flat on my back on the wooden floor. I looked up to see four people hovering over me – Alison, Sachiko, the chef, and his helper. Alison ran to the kitchen for ice cubes and a plastic bag to cover my ankle, my first ever broken bone.

I lay sprawled on the floor blocking the front door, concentrating on taking slow deep breaths to keep from fainting from the shooting pain in my foot. Within minutes Sachiko's guests arrived for her party. I looked up at their inquiring faces and had to say something. "Hello, I'm Sachi's American sister. I'm sorry to be welcoming you from down here." I hoped I didn't sound as miserable as I felt. My throbbing ankle was only part of my pain. I had just ruined Sachiko's party.

Alison didn't leave my side. When Sachiko's son, Masa, arrived, he drove us to the closest urgent care facility. It was an older building with no elevators and all the doctors' offices on the second floor. I wondered what people in wheelchairs did. Leaning heavily on Masa on one side and Alison on the other, we labored up the stairs. After an interminable wait in the crowded waiting room, we learned the doctor had no way to x-ray my foot. He referred me to the Emergency Department of Scarborough General, the closest hospital, so we edged down the stairs, into the car, and on to the hospital. My broken ankle was about to make me a card-carrying member of the Canadian health system. Four hours later, I emerged with my lower leg and ankle in a plaster cast, with strict instructions not to put any weight on that foot, and to keep it raised above my heart, an impossible request. They gave me crutches that were so large, they were useless. Back at Sachiko's, the guests were waiting to see me before leaving.

Alison showed me how to get upstairs to the bedroom by sitting backwards and lifting my rear from one step to the next, a technique she had learned after a high school volleyball injury. She helped me get undressed and into bed. Without her, I would have been helpless. Finally in bed, it was time to call home. I could feel myself starting to let down; no need to maintain my cheerful front. Alison called Russ to tell him what happened while I tried to compose myself. I wanted to sound matter-of-fact so I didn't worry him, but when she handed me the phone, uncontrollable sobs escaped. Russ could only listen helplessly to my blubbering.

The next morning, I sat in the backseat with my leg up while Sachiko drove us to the hotel where we would be staying for the next two nights. Our goodbyes were awkward. I rarely got to see Sachi and this was not the visit we had wanted. Embarrassed, and both feeling responsible for my accident, neither of us knew what to say.

After checking in at the hotel, Alison and I sat in our hotel room, discussing how to tackle our business obligations for the next two days.

"You said you were coming as my baggage handler," I told her. "That turned out to be prophetic. I can't even get my clothes out of my suitcase without you. Will you take my place at the meeting with our importer this morning? I'd like to stay here with my foot up to be ready for this afternoon." Alison's smile showed that she was pleased with the responsibility.

"I can do it, Mom," she said, and off she went.

I had to host the Sokol Blosser Winery dinner that night at one of Toronto's best restaurants, called Jamie Kennedy at the Gardiner. Every guest would receive a signed copy of my newly published book and I was to read excerpts between courses. That was not something I could delegate. I looked optimistically at my new crutches, hoping I could learn to use them quickly.

My first crutch management lesson came when our importer drove us to Jamie Kennedy's restaurant for lunch. Unable to attend the dinner since he was being honored as Restaurateur of the Year that evening, Jamie had invited us for lunch to see the space and have a chance to chat. I started up the wheelchair ramp to the entrance, woefully underestimating how much strength crutches demanded. Before I was halfway to the door, my shoulders and arms ached and I was panting. Once inside, we had a thirty foot walk to the elevator. A distance I normally wouldn't have noticed seemed endless, and beads of sweat threatened to cascade down my flushed face. When we finally reached the dining room, I sat down and put my throbbing foot up on a chair, not caring how it looked. We put the wines we had brought for Jamie to taste on the table, set up the tasting, and ordered lunch. I looked longingly as the wine was poured, but it was the last thing I needed in my already wobbly state.

Jamie Kennedy had been a featured chef at the Monterey Bay Aquarium's Cooking for Solutions when I first met him. He had told me he loved Pinot Noir, so when arranging our Toronto trip, I contacted him and he invited me to do a winery dinner at his new restaurant on the third floor of the Gardiner Museum. Our lunch gave me the chance to see the light, airy space and discuss the logistics of table arrangement, menu, wine pairing, and how the courses would flow. After lunch, lurching back to the elevator, out the front door, and down the ramp again, left me limp and weary. I couldn't face doing it again that evening for the dinner. In my pained state, a wheelchair sounded divine. We asked at the hotel desk. Yes, the hotel had one wheelchair; they would let us borrow it for the day. The concierge disappeared, reappearing five minutes later pushing a dusty, rickety-looking, bare bones wheelchair. It had no adjustments, but just seeing the wheels turn improved my mood immediately. It fell to Alison to roll me around. I couldn't imagine what I'd have done if I'd been alone.

When we returned to the restaurant in the evening, the dining room looked splendid. Our plan was that I'd talk about the wines and read from my book between courses. The podium I had requested, with microphone and light, stood well positioned to see the entire dining room. A podium allowed me to rest the book while I read. The microphone preserved my voice. Additional light was necessary to read in a darkened restaurant ambiance. At noon, when I still thought I would be able to stand, these were important. By evening, reduced to a wheelchair, none were of use. Our last minute revision gave Alison the chance for another first.

"Alison," I asked, "Can you go up to the podium and talk to the group about the wines?" She hadn't filled in for me like this before but she knew the wines. It would be a good opportunity for her.

"I can do it," she said.

"After you talk about the wines, maybe you'd introduce me. Then I'll start reading." She nodded. I continued. "Are you willing to go around to the tables and talk to the guests and answer any questions?" I asked her. This would be harder.

"Okay," she said, with just a slight hesitation.

The break in my ankle became the break Alison needed to push her to perform presidentially in public. Hiding any nervousness, she did a fine job talking about the wines and introducing me. I watched as she went around "working the tables," talking to the guests. Gracious and smiling, she rose to her role. This was a big step for her, and for me as well, letting her do what I had always done. Focused on my presentation, I didn't think about it at the time, but the baton was starting to switch hands.

After considering the alternatives, none of them good, I decided to read sitting at the table, from my wheelchair – no microphone, no light, and at the same level as the seated guests. I could engage my audience from a podium, but this unusual situation made me nervous. My fears dissipated as I got into a rhythm. I could feel everyone's attention. There was still enough daylight coming in from the three glass walls of the restaurant, which jutted out like a peninsula, to see the print easily. Dusk ended that. After the second course, when it was time for the next reading, the restaurant was dark, lit only by votive candles on the tables. The effect was lovely, but the only way to see the print on the page was to prop the book at my place setting and surround it with candles. My table mates collected votives and I did the next two readings by candlelight. It felt like we were sitting around a campfire and I was telling stories.

To everyone's surprise, this unconventional presentation ended up having a special magic. Our importer reported that weeks later people were still talking about it. The manager of a private club, who was one of the diners, pleaded with me to come back and do a wine and book reading dinner for his members. He was even willing to let me read by candlelight. We smiled all the way back to the hotel. Everyone was happy: I with relief that I had fulfilled my obligation; Alison with pleasure at succeeding in her new role; our importer with all the wine that was sold. After one more event, Alison and I headed home. I couldn't wait to get to an orthopedist's office to learn how long I would be laid up. The Canadian doctor who had examined me said about six weeks. The young man who put me in a cast confirmed this. Out of commission for six weeks! I asked if there was anything I could do to accelerate healing, like vitamins I could take, or foods I could eat.

"Sardines," he said immediately. "Because they are rich in calcium to help your bones mend. Of course, I'm Portuguese," he explained. "We eat many sardines."

Sardines had not been in my diet for years, but they immediately went on my mental shopping list. I was in good health; maybe, with enough sardines, I could be back in action in five. Wrong. Even after I was walking again, I was in physical therapy for several months.

Losing my office no longer mattered. I couldn't get up the stairs to the offices. I tried, but didn't have the upper body strength to hoist myself up and down multiple times a day on crutches. Russ suggested I work from home and arranged for a network satellite on the winery building to be hooked to our home computer. We were about to add on and remodel the winery offices. By the time I healed, I would have my own office again.

I spent April and May working from home. My cast gave way to a large unwieldy boot that felt like a ball and chain. Alex and Alison were negotiating to buy an additional fifteen acres of vineyard land, dubbed Blackberry Block as it was overrun with invasive Himalayan Blackberries. Normally, I would have been walking all over it, examining the soil and slope. But walking on bumpy, uneven ground was out of the question for close to three months. For weeks, even navigating the grocery store with Russ was too much for me. No vineyard walks. No driving. The physical limitations made me grumpy. I wanted to be out and about.

The quiet serenity of my office at home, broken only by the sound of the birds and the creek outside my window, started to change my outlook. Little golden finches splashed brightly in the stream, the drops sparkling as they fluttered through their bath. I could work at my computer, make phone calls, go make a cup of tea, admire the spring flowers, watch the water tumble over the rocks, then work some more.

At the end of May, looking up from my home computer at the little waterfall outside the office window, I realized what had happened. While I wasn't at the winery on a daily basis, my two children took charge. They relied on each other and handled the crises as well as day-to-day operations. The staff got used to me not being around and regularly looked to Alex and Alison for leadership. I started to be at peace with Alex handling the vineyard and production and Alison handling financial accounting and administration. I was grateful they were running the vineyard and winery, glad not to have to appear at an office every morning, and relieved they were dealing with the never-ending issues that made each day a challenge. I could finally feel the bonds loosening.

The universe had stepped in to move me off my plateau, forcing me forward with a swift, well-placed kick. All things considered, it was done in the kindest way: in a familial, caring setting, and a clean break, no displacement or surgery needed. Just enough to remove me from the frontline for almost two months. It took a physical act, but the resistance that had dragged on for so long, started to release. I had no idea what the future held, but I had the sense I was creating a place for it to grow. My ankle episode, though painful, embarrassing, and inelegant, turned out to be a pivotal part of the transition.

With the practice year half over, I should be celebrating that I was finally at the point where I was not only willing, but thankful to have Alex and Alison taking over. The pace I had kept up for so many years now seemed too hurried, too hard to keep up. I wanted to move more slowly and do less in a day. It didn't feel like old age, rather like moving on. The vineyards and winery were in my blood, but I was ready for something new. I didn't want to exchange one level of frenetic activity for another and had a mental image of myself lying on my back, floating, in the middle of a lake. I'd left one shore, was part way to the other side, and wanted to relax before stroking again.

When the winery and vineyard were my total focus, business dictated the structure of my life. Now, with no schedule to keep and the world wide open, I didn't know which way to turn. Was this what retirement meant? The fatigue I'd resisted had worked its way to consciousness. I felt tired to the bone. Tired of pushing myself so hard, of making business my first priority, of having to be serious all the time. My exhaustion wasn't physical, it was emotional. Once I was able to get around again, I found myself wanting to garden all day, annoyed at having to stop to meet some business deadline.

On one of our conferences, Marsia admonished me to let myself be tired and not spoil it with judgment and fear of doing the wrong thing. She rattled off six R words, convincing me what I should be doing: resting, reflecting, refreshing, renewing, rejuvenating, recalibrating. The void I felt was part of the process of letting go. She assured me a new passion would come when it was time. There was no need to feel guilty at not being more productive. Couldn't I let myself vegetate for a while? Accepting her R words as a remedy pitted my desire to follow her advice against my innate pressure to be productive.

Compelled to do something to get myself out of my mental muddle, I bought ***The Artist's Way***, by Julia Cameron, and forced myself to do the recommended exercises, following the path to what the author called "creative recovery." The author emphasized two of the exercises as "pivotal tools in creative recovery." The first, a daily writing of "Morning Pages," entailed moving your hand across the page to write, without stopping to censor or edit until you had three pages. I had no trouble doing this and made a ritual of sitting down each morning to let flow what I was thinking about, what was happening that day, my frustrations, fears, hopes. That notebook records a picture of my inner life during that turbulent time as the winery slowly receded. Rather than expounding on winery issues, my Morning Pages for the summer of 2007 were filled with entries of excitement for my new garden, appreciation for the birds around our home, frustration with my mother, caring for Alex's twin boys, concern for Russ's back pain, and only occasionally winery issues. By the end of August I was able to write, "I'm feeling less and less interested in the wine business." I felt guilty writing that, but I had come to realize that in order to let go, I had to care less.

The second task was called "artist's date." This was a weekly play date, but only with yourself. The author gave strict instructions to go alone on the artist's date. "That means no lovers, friends, spouses, children – no taggers-on of any stripe," she admonished. I failed miserably on this assignment. Despite loving the idea of thinking of something I wanted to do and scheduling time to do it, my mind went blank at the thought of "playing." I couldn't think of anything I wanted to do enough to do it alone. The difficulty I had was a clue how much inner self I let atrophy in pursuit of business success. The closest I came was gardening, although I didn't do it alone. That was the summer Russ and I started a vegetable garden, something I hadn't done for over twenty years. Russ built raised beds for me and we bought strawberry and raspberry plants, heirloom tomatoes, and seeds galore. I puttered happily in the dirt. My new garden didn't erase my focus on the vineyard, but it became the pinch-hitter. At the family board meeting at my house that July, the first item on the agenda was a "Tour of Mom's new raised beds," with 15 minutes allotted.

My job description finally took shape. Alison helped me combine Pat's concerns with my indecision on how involved I wanted to be. The result was short and simple. As Founder my job was to be an ambassador for the vineyards and winery, participating in projects to further the vision, mission, and goals of the business. Its vagueness appealed to me. I would have the freedom to get as involved as I chose. It made me clearly subordinate and reporting to the co-presidents. Alex and Alison would sign my employee paycheck and my expense reports. I would live with that new reality when I passed the baton. Another piece of the transition was in place.

I enjoyed telling people that, at the end of the transition, my kids would be signing my expense reimbursement checks. It always drew a chuckle. To me it symbolized a real transfer of power. Phasing out of being the "face" of the winery and letting Alex and Alison take that role was also important. Keeping the public mantle didn't seem fair, although it was common practice in family businesses. If the kids were running the business, they should represent it publicly. Alex and Alison were both first-rate winery ambassadors. The transition would be complete when their prominence eclipsed mine and I'd be introduced as their mother, rather than the other way around.

The family suggested I be Chair of the Board, another frequent practice for retiring CEOs. I chose not to do that. Nik, the only child not earning a living at the winery, had agreed to lead the family board and it was a perfect role for him. Being chair engaged him more fully in the business. Time would show how valuable his strategic mind would be to us. As one of the new generation of young entrepreneurs, his experience with his own company provided constructive perspective. In view of my penchant for control, I needed to bow out completely for the transition to work.

9

Mother

My mother never became actively involved in the winery business, but that was the only part of my life she didn't try to control or manipulate. I didn't understand why our relationship was so difficult as she was exactly the kind of person I would choose as a friend: an independent thinker, good sense of humor, outgoing, engaged with life. But as my mother, a different dynamic predominated. She held the key to my security and happiness. A counselor had told me once, during couples therapy with Bill, that I was "a pleaser." The phrase was new to me but touched something inside. I immediately understood.

"Be yourself," he told me. "Let the cards fall where they may." He looked at Bill as he said to me, "If your husband doesn't like it, that's his problem. Don't try to change to accommodate him." A shudder of fear went through me hearing his advice. While I knew what he meant, I couldn't do it.

I learned to be a "pleaser" as a child, seeking approval from my charismatic mother. If I wanted her love, I needed to make her happy. How I felt or what I wanted didn't matter. But pleasing her conflicted with the drive to be myself. I wanted my mother to love me for who I was, not her image of the ideal daughter. The result was I alternated between trying to become the daughter she envisioned and resisting the pressure to conform.

Because she encouraged and praised extroverted activity, I felt free to develop the outer, public me. But pleasing my mother, and later my husband, had unfortunate consequences. When given the chance to be myself, I floundered indecisively. When I left Bill, at the age of fifty-four, I still knew little about who I was when I wasn't trying to please someone.

As a teenager, I rebelled by applying for the American Field Service student exchange and going to Japan. I was attending Milwaukee Downer Seminary, a girls' school where my classmates came from prominent manufacturing and banking families. They had cute nicknames, like Bitsy, Missy, TT, Babby, Candy, Squeaky, Tiny. At public school, I was at the top of the socio-economic ladder. At Downer, I was at the bottom. Susie Sokol could only secure a place in the hierarchy by performance, either athletic or academic. Fortunately, I liked both.

I got straight A's in school although neither parent paid much attention to my grades. I asked my mother why, especially when I saw my friends get rewarded when they got good marks. "We expect you to get A's," she told me, articulating what I had known inside; the bar for me was set higher. Trying to meet that standard became the stage where my life played out.

After my senior year in high school, she took me to France to attend the summer session for foreigners at the University of Grenoble. As a result of my previous summer in Japan, I had decided to go into Japanese studies, partly because I had fallen in love with a Japanese college student. This situation, which she discovered by surreptitiously reading some of his letters to me, horrified her. She wanted to shift my focus westward, so taking me to France was a strategic move. It worked. I came home speaking French and pursued it in college, instead of my intended Japanese.

During the summer of 1962 in France, we lived in the historic part of Grenoble, with a widow in an arrangement called a pension. We and four other Americans, all college students, stayed with Madame Michoud in her large apartment. We took meals at her long dining table, speaking French with American accents ranging from southern to midwestern. It was a brave thing for my fifty-seven year old mother to do, spending a summer rooming with her teenage daughter, who made it clear what a burden it was to be with her mother.

We each attended French conversation classes. The rest of the time I did my best to distance myself. The other Americans, just a little older than I, seemed to love to be with my mother. She was so popular that two of the young women, college students in Illinois, came to visit us in Milwaukee after we returned. Their attraction baffled me since I found her mostly annoying.

My classmates had followed school tradition and looked at women's colleges in the northeastern United States. I decided to go west to a coed school and chose California, as far away from my home and the stultifying culture of an upper middle class girls' school as I could get.

Mother and I remained locked in dance position, with her leading. I didn't think I could both please her and be myself. My insides churned at the standards I thought she had for how I should dress, act, marry, and raise children. I say "thought" as I never asked, just made assumptions about what she wanted, based on the clues she gave me. When my daughter, Alison, became a teenager and requested that I not come in, but wait in the car when I picked her up at a school function, I thought of my teenage years when my mother was my embarrassment. The phrase "divine retribution" sprang to mind.

My marriage to Bill underlined my emotional dilemma. I got caught in the crosshairs of trying to please both Bill and Mother. Their power struggle dated from our wedding, a battle of wills over whether Bill would wear the new suit he had bought for the occasion or the white dinner jacket my mother insisted was proper wedding attire. There was no bringing them together. Each was determined to win, Bill on principle, mother on propriety. She had an image in her mind of how her daughter's wedding should look. It never occurred to me that she may have wanted the wedding she had been denied, married during the Depression by a Justice of the Peace.

When Mother and I shopped for a wedding dress, she pointed to an extravagant dress with a long train. Bill had told me he didn't want a fancy wedding, explicitly requesting a dress with no train. I chose what I thought was a compromise, a simple linen wedding dress with a slightly elongated rear skirt, forming a mini train. It was too much for Bill and not enough for mother. Such a small thing, but emotions ran high. Both were annoyed and I was miserable. In trying to find a middle ground, I had pleased neither.

The dress may have been what made Bill put his foot down on wearing his dark blue suit instead of a white dinner jacket. "I've given in on everything else," he told me. "Your mother's pushed me far enough. I'm going to take a stand on this one." Trying to please both, an impossible task, left me disheartened and depressed at a time that should have been joyful. Mother got my brothers to work on Bill and made sure the jacket was rented so it would be ready when they succeeded, which she knew they would. I do not have good memories of either the wedding or reception, although my mother was thrilled with both and always spoke of it as the party of the century. My oldest brother's wife explained to me later: "Your mistake is that you thought this was your wedding."

The wedding conflict didn't end my childhood pattern. I just changed my focus to pleasing my husband rather than my mother. With no finish line, I was always striving, never good enough. The strain of trying to be the person I thought Bill wanted me to be, kept me in a state of perpetual self-criticism. I never saw the paradox of wanting to be loved for who I was, while I was trying to be someone else. Counseling, our business, and three children at the center of both our worlds, kept us together for over thirty years.

I have met a number of women of my generation who, like me, were strong and high achieving in their careers but submissive and self-effacing in intimate relationships. We started out modeling ourselves on the cultural norms of our childhood, then, as we came of age in the 1960s and 70s, embraced feminism. Our career breakthroughs, however difficult, were easier to achieve than reshaping male-female relationships. My mother, who told me she was making more money than my father when she married, followed convention to quit her career and stay home when she had children. She did what was expected. Proper respectability was a core value of her age. My generation broke that mold.

My college roommates and I loved the songs from the musical, ***The Fantasticks***, whose words spoke to our hopes and dreams. "Please, God, please, don't let me be normal...I want much more than keeping house, much more, muuuch more!" We didn't know what we wanted, but we knew what we didn't want. As we entered adulthood, Gloria Steinem's charge, "A woman needs a man like a fish needs a bicycle," rang in our ears.

Mother and Daddy moved to McMinnville in 1980. I never quite understood why Mother chose to live near me rather than one of my brothers, since she was always talking about how wonderful they were. For the rest of her life, she lived nearby but kept in touch with my brothers and made sure we knew the latest about each other and our children. After Daddy died, her authority as head of the family increased. I tried to see or at least talk to her once a week. We could discuss politics, literature, hobbies, food, and family. I chose my subjects carefully to avoid her judgment.

When she had turned eighty, although in good health, I knew that she was at an age when any moment could be her last. I tried to see her regularly, although my life was full of demands and I often longed to be elsewhere. That went on for twenty-two years. When she turned 98, I began to think she would live forever.

In her mid-nineties, she decided she needed a new car and told me with a mischievous grin: "The car dealer tried to talk me into buying by promising me free oil changes for life." She laughed. "He figures I'm going to die soon and he got a good deal." My brothers and I chuckled that the car dealer would soon learn the joke was on him. I called her the "energizer bunny." She listened to classical music daily, turning up the volume over time as her hearing got worse. She had given her grand piano to my musical brother, Henry, but missed playing, so when she was almost 100, she rented a piano, playing every day, as much as her arthritic hands would allow. "I always start with 'The Jolly Farmer,'" she told me. I can hear her playing it now, cheerful and upbeat, her bright red nails clicking on the piano key. Evenings, in her nightgown and robe, she sat at her computer to check her email, do a daily jigsaw puzzle, and play a game of computer solitaire before bed.

She weathered a heart valve replacement and breast cancer with optimism and aplomb. Finally tired of cooking, she searched for compatible women who came to the house during the day and cooked her meals. She hired them based on their intelligence, how well they played Scrabble, and their cooking. Scrabble proficiency trumped cooking. I remember her telling me that she kept one woman on, even though her food wasn't very good, because she was such a good Scrabble player. Mother didn't start live-in care until she was over 100. Her caretakers were devoted to her.

The Christmas after she had turned 100, Russ and I took Mother to Nik's house for a late morning brunch and gift giving. Our extended family had come together, including Bill, our children and grandchildren, aunts and uncles. We sat around the edge of Nik's large living room, the grandchildren in the middle, close to the presents. The floor was strewn with crumpled Christmas wrap and children's toys, making it impossible to move. Nik played Santa Claus. He sat next to the tree, picked up each present, and read who it was for. Most were for the grandchildren, but then he called out my name. I watched a small square package make its way from under the large decorated Christmas tree, hand to hand over to me. When I unwrapped and opened the box, I looked at Mother, who was crying. Inside, nestled in velvet, were the antique gold brooch, bracelet, and ring decorated with tiny pearls and turquoise that her grandmother had brought with her from Russia. I read the note she had included in the box: "I'm passing these to you as the next matriarch of the family." Then I started crying too.

Mother didn't slow down as she aged. After she moved to McMinnville in her mid-seventies, she organized a group of local women to meet for conversation and handwork which she called the 'Knit Pickers'; she started a Mahjong group and played bridge twice a week; she had weekly golf games, not cutting back from eighteen to nine holes until she was in her nineties. She followed national politics with great interest, watched TV news nightly, and never missed watching Tim Russert on "Meet the Press." She loved to talk politics and lived for political debate. Her eyes sparkled when she sparred with her conservative Republican friends every Sunday over brunch after church. I'd hear about these jousts on my Sunday visits. She stopped attending live theater, the symphony, and opera, but was never without a book to read. She traveled to visit friends and family. When one project ended, she devised another. She always had something to look forward to.

Her independent streak had come into full flower when my father's Alzheimer's got out of control and she could no longer care for him at home. She was eighty-two when he died and couldn't understand why so many of her friends who lost a husband at her age immediately latched onto another man. "Why do they insist on finding a replacement?" she said. "They'll just end up having to take care of him." She continued to live alone with her cat, relishing her freedom. Her window of life never narrowed.

She loved to have people guess her age. She looked so much younger than she was and delighted in the surprised looks when she revealed it. Surprisingly unwrinkled and with a thick head of hair, she didn't seem to me to look "old" until she was in her late 90s. When people exclaimed about her age, she'd quip "only the good die young." She acknowledged how little time she had left with "I don't even buy green bananas anymore."

Then, in the middle of the transition practice year, 2007, her health failed. Her mind was still sharp, but her heart valve developed a leak. She started having occasional episodes when her lungs filled with fluid, stressing her heart, and producing panic as she struggled to breathe. Her caretakers, now round the clock, would take her to the hospital. She'd be back home in a day or two, full of life, but she was in her 102nd year. Her body had finally succumbed and was slowly giving out, although the feisty, opinionated joking never wavered. I telephoned her when told she was hospitalized early in July. When she recognized my voice she responded in her best Bugs Bunny imitation, "Well, isn't this a revoltin' development!"

That year she grew physically smaller as her appetite diminished. I told her she reminded me of the Cheshire cat in ***Alice in Wonderland***, who disappeared little by little until all that was left was his grin. She said she wouldn't mind being remembered as a smile. She accepted her smaller personage as part of getting old, while she remained focused on living. I didn't have the courage to talk to her about dying and she never brought it up. But the signs were there. She started spending most of the day on the couch with her feet on a footstool, reading nonfiction, playing Scrabble, visiting with friends, and watching the national news on TV, seldom leaving home. Watching President George W. Bush always got her adrenalin going. Anger at his politics kept her blood circulating. She continued her routine, still winning money at Mahjong every Tuesday, although her friends now came to her house to play.

The beginning of the end came when one of her episodes included a mini-stroke. Her speech slurred and she had difficulty walking. Home from the hospital, she gradually spoke more clearly but breathing was so uncomfortable she slept sitting up on the couch with pillows. She didn't want to eat, and needed her oxygen, first every night, then all day as well. Her doctor put her back in the hospital where, he told me, they'd "have more tools to make her feel better."

Staying in her own home had been a high priority, so I knew she must be feeling awful to agree to leave. She had briefly considered moving to a retirement home after Daddy died, but decided to stay put. "I don't want to be with all those old people," she explained. She was proud to remain in her home with all the things she loved, counting the grosbeaks at her feeders and enjoying the colorful roses on her deck, her cat snuggled up next to her.

She entered the hospital suddenly again, the night of July 18, 2007. Early the next morning, I had a physical therapy appointment for my ankle at the hospital and went to see her in the Intensive Care Unit right afterwards, before starting a day full of appointments. She was sleeping, on oxygen and IV's, and looked small and shrunken, her face almost skeletal with hollow cheeks and sunken eyes. This could be the beginning of the end; maybe my mother was finally going to die. I'd given up trying to be with her as much as I knew she wanted. More than once, I guiltily wished she would make her exit. I wondered if then I would be free from her judgmental voice that lived in my mind.

The hospital doctor, an unusually jolly man who resembled Santa Claus ("call me Dr. D," he said) talked to me while she slept. He said she was so weak she couldn't suck water up through the straw. Her heart was failing and her lungs kept filling with fluid, making breathing difficult to the point of panic. He had put her on a small dose of morphine to allay the panic and would "tune her up a bit," whatever that meant. Then she could go home, probably under a hospice situation. He said it casually, but his words went right through me. We had never spoken about hospice.

Mother opened her eyes when her breakfast arrived. I fed her two tiny bites of egg, then a piece of a fresh strawberry before she closed her mouth firmly, rejecting more. Trying to feed my mother shook me to the core. I told her I loved her. She whispered she loved me, then told me to take anything I wanted from her home and closed her eyes.

A subtle change had occurred. My mother, who loved life, knew she was not going back home. I was in tears by the time I got back to the car, too distraught to face a wine industry board meeting in an hour. I could cancel that, but I couldn't cancel the speech I was scheduled to deliver that afternoon at a Key Bank for Women program. Mother, a performer herself, had taught me that the show must go on.

Back at the winery, I told Alison how upsetting seeing Grandma Phyllis had been. She comforted me with a hug and asked if I wanted her to go with me to Portland for moral support. I instinctively said, "No, I'll be fine," then admitted I needed her help. She cancelled her own appointments and drove me to Portland. Steeling myself to focus on what I had to do, I managed to forget for an hour that my mother could be dying at that very moment.

When Alison and I visited Mother later that afternoon, we found her almost cheery. Why had I jumped to the conclusion she was dying? Here she was, rebounding like always. She had visitors and phone calls and talked clearly. Although weak, she showed us she was now able to drink through a straw. I debated what, if anything to tell my brothers. I'd worried them in previous episodes over the past few months, when she'd gone to the hospital in the middle of the night because she couldn't breathe, then she bounced back and was as good as ever. Alison reminded me that I couldn't know what the outcome would be. "You need to give them the facts," my organized, rational daughter advised. "It could be their last chance to come to see her and say goodbye." I went home and called them.

The others couldn't get away, but Henry took the first plane he could from Milwaukee. He arrived the next morning. Henry hadn't seen Mother for many months and couldn't believe the change. He had wanted to sit by her bedside and hold her hand, but couldn't do it. "I had to leave the room," he told me. "I couldn't bear to see her."

By Sunday morning, when several of us went to visit, I knew a deathwatch had begun. She appeared asleep despite eyes open in a glassy-eyed stare. Her moving chest indicated she was still alive, but she looked like a ghost. We had come for a short visit, but I decided to stay with her. It wasn't a question of "ought" or "should" this time. I simply knew to stay. People trickled in all day to see how she was and to say goodbye. Mother lay with her eyes closed, not responding to any of the bustle around her.

Late in the day, while Alison and I were sitting at Mother's bedside, we looked up with surprise as a woman wearing a royal blue shirt with a starched white cleric's collar strode in. "Hi, I'm Priest Kathleen from St. Barnabas Episcopal Church." Mother had mentioned months before that the new priest at her church was a woman, and here she was, cheerfully pulling up her chair close to the bed. She started talking to Mother in everyday conversational tones, then did a short service of prayer, ending with the Twenty-third Psalm. Mother's eyes remained closed the whole time, but when we saw her lips move in response to hearing her favorite psalm, we knew she had been following, her first physical response of the day.

Priest Kathleen told us what a wonderful journey mother was on and how honored she, Kathleen, felt to be witnessing it. Her indication that death was a beginning, rather than an end, was new information. Before she walked out, Priest Kathleen suggested we tell stories and relive memorable moments with our mother and grandma who, she assured us, was listening. "That will help her, and you too," Kathleen advised. Alison and I looked at each other and hesitantly, weeping as we thought of old times, forced ourselves to start talking.

We had arranged another family gathering that evening, but I couldn't leave mother. After years of trying to avoid being with her,

I felt myself rooted to her inert but still living body. No one was with me. Russ had been away on a trip with his mother and sister during the past two weeks and wasn't expected home for another twenty-four hours. Dr. D. came by for the daily report. He told me mother had gone downhill fast, that her kidneys were shutting down, and that she probably only had between six and twenty-four hours left. He said she might not make it through the night. Hospice would not be necessary. I took a deep breath and let it out slowly. Not only was this the end, but it could be soon.

Then it was just Mother and me in the hospital room. I had never been this close to death before. My grandparents all died before I was born; my father died before my mother and I could reach his bedside. Witnessing death would be a new frontier, one I would face alone, nervous but riveted.

Alex appeared unexpectedly after dinner with a deck of cards, a CD player and some classical music. "I thought Grandma would like to listen to music," he said. His thoughtfulness touched me and I was glad for his company. We put on Mozart's Requiem and played gin rummy for an hour before he went home.

The nurse who came in to check on Mother told me what to expect. "Listen for changes," she told me. I stretched out on the chair bed, sleeping fitfully as the night sounds of the hospital kept intruding. Every time I woke I monitored Mother's breathing. At 4:30, as day broke and the sky lightened, I got up. As my mother lay motionless on the bed, I sat close to her and started talking about her parents, her Grandma Richter, her husband Gus, her friends who had died – all the people she loved who were waiting for her. I assured her that Ronnie, her attorney son, would take care of everything. Her cat would have a good home. If Dr. D was right, she didn't have much time left. His twenty-four hour prediction would be up in a few hours.

Mother foiled Dr. D's prediction. Nervous with anticipation, relief spread through me when Priest Kathleen appeared, later in the day. "I'm just sitting here waiting for her to die," I told her. "How long will this go on?" "She'll go when she's ready," Kathleen said. Mother's favorite caretaker had called and offered to stay the night with her. I went back home to be with Russ who had just returned from his family trip through Canada. When I returned the next morning, Mother seemed to be in a deeper sleep but I saw no other change. Although her breathing was regular, my gut told me the end was near. I sat next to the head of the bed and tried to read, but my eyes kept returning to my mother's face. I watched as her throat muscles relaxed and she started gurgling. Dr. D. had told me that this sound, the famous death rattle, was uncomfortable to listen to but not painful for the patient. Two attendants came in to give Mother a quick bath, change her gown and reposition her. What a little thing she had become. She moaned a little but didn't awake. Sometimes her eyes opened and she seemed to be staring up into the distance. With uncanny timing, Priest Kathleen appeared and sat with me.

"Have you been at many deathbeds?" I asked her. She recounted some of her experiences, including her own near-death experience. "We celebrate birth," she said, "because we know the possibilities ahead. We don't celebrate death because we don't see the possibilities, but they are there, just in another realm, another world, another dimension. We can look back on youth; no one can look back on old age." Watching Mother over the course of her five days in the hospital, I understood that we labor to die, just as we labor to birth. I'd never considered how analogous the two processes were.

Kathleen stood next to the bed and recited the Twenty-third Psalm twice and the Lord's Prayer one more time. She told Mother to reach out to the loved ones welcoming her when she was ready, that it was okay to go. We talked a little longer. I asked her why mother's eyes were open. She said Mother was deep in her journey and was likely seeing things. It wasn't uncommon, she explained, for people near death to suddenly sit up or move their legs as if walking. They're responding to something they're seeing and wanting to move towards. I was glad she'd explained that as I'd have panicked if mother suddenly sat up. "It won't be long now," Kathleen said as she left. "Watch her face for clues."

I closed the door to the room to shut out hospital noise and sat close to the bed, watching for changes. I wondered what Mother saw, as flickers of recognition seemed to pass across her face, showing more expression than it had the last two days. Her breathing got slower and slower. Twenty minutes after Kathleen gave her last words of encouragement, Mother took her last breath. I felt the energy in the room shift as her spirit rose and crossed into another dimension, leaving a lifeless body behind. It was a blessed moment. I would never think of death the same again and understood what Priest Kathleen meant when she said it was an honor to be present. How lucky to have the chance to die like this, to be able to say goodbye to people from this life, and have loved ones sit with you while you slowly make your way to the next one. Those who die suddenly, without warning, whether quietly or violently, don't receive this luxury.

I sat with Mother for a few minutes before calling the winery. Alex answered and said he would come immediately to be with me. In the silence before he arrived, I thought about how, in the last twenty years, Mother had shown me how to live, growing old with grace, humor, and independence. Now she had shown me how to die, gently and serenely. The complications that made our relationship difficult – the uncomfortable critiques and unreasonable demands – were no longer important. I knew she loved me. She knew I loved her. We were bound together through many dimensions and lifetimes. The issues we had in this life were minor by comparison. The rawness of our relationship kept me from wanting her back, but her death left a surprisingly deep hole in my heart.

After Mother died, before my brother Ronnie, who was her executor, came from his home in France to deal with the estate, I felt pulled to her house. I went alone and never stayed long, just wandered through the rooms, taking in what remained of her. The house sat silent and still, her things just as she left them. Her smell lingered, as if she were just out for a walk and would soon return.

She would not have thought of leaving home without make-up and nail polish. Bottles of bright red polish and lipsticks to match stood ready to use, next to her hairbrush, filled with white hair. A row of colorful no-iron shirts hung ready for action in her large walk-in closet, along with favorite dresses she had kept over the years, some in dress bags, others hanging on padded satin hangers. The dresses were full of memories, each one associated with a special party, a wedding, or a family dinner. Her pink fleece bathrobe with the long zipper down the front making it easy to step into, hung on a hook next to the bathroom door.

Family pictures smiled out from her dresser – formal wedding shots of grandchildren and more casual ones of my brothers and me. On the nightstand next to her bed lay the book she had been reading, a political critique of George W. Bush. The white rose afghan I had crocheted for her years ago lay sprawled across the foot of the bed. Her computer screen, where she played her nightly game of solitaire before climbing in bed, sat dark and silent in the corner of the room.

On the deck her bird feeders sat empty and the roses needed water. I watered them, then, over the next month, brought the rose planters home and created my own little rose garden, a memorial to Mother's love of flowers.

Her presence lingered until my brother Ronnie arrived with his oldest son and their cigar smoke changed the tenor of the house. By then I was willing to move on, although part of me wished I could capture her scent, a perfume I'd never much liked and whose name I'd forgotten, but which I found myself oddly missing.

I immediately arranged a memorial service at Mother's church. I knew my brothers couldn't get away on short notice but I felt I owed it to Mother and the community to do something right away. Mother had a large circle of friends, although she had outlived her age group. As her old friends slipped away one by one, younger women took their place. When she died, her friends were in their eighties, old women but still twenty years younger than she. I saw the vibrancy of her friendships in her photo albums, which recorded numerous get-togethers of fashionable, carefully coiffed, smiling women playing bridge or Mahjong, blowing out birthday candles on cakes decorated with roses and violets, and enjoying field trips. At her memorial service they filled the Episcopal Church. I spoke as the only one of her children in attendance, stifling a sob as I began.

My brothers and I planned for our families to get together several months later, in October. We would have a big dinner with memories and toasts and a small ceremony at the cemetery. Ronnie, as her executor, came early to take care of all her things. There was so much stuff. I was glad to let him deal with it. Russ's and my relatively small home could not accept any more dishes, furniture, or art. Some things had sentimental value, but nothing of great worth. I already possessed what meant most to me, primarily the samovar my great grandmother had brought with her when she emigrated from Russia. Ronnie spread everything out on display and invited the grandchildren and great grandchildren to take what they wanted. I passed up everything, even the pastel chalk childhood portrait of me, which had been hanging in the family home as long as I could remember, even though mother always said she was never really happy with it. What wasn't taken was sold at a garage sale. I lost track of where it all went.

A few big pieces of furniture that didn't sell stayed in the house, which was rented for four years before it finally sold and we had to remove everything. At that point, I was setting up my office in McMinnville and found a way to use mother's old secretary desk and the two Queen Anne wingback chairs which had been part of my childhood. Even her decorative lacquered Asian pieces found a place in my new office. All the things that wouldn't have fit in my current home made my office warm and cozy. When visitors commented on the homey decor, I told them I had recreated my mother's living room.

One day, in the process of setting up my office, I wandered through a local antique mall in search of a coat rack. Turning a corner I found myself face to face with my childhood portrait hanging on a wall. I wondered what path it had taken to get there and stood frozen on the spot, riveted by my four year old self staring back at me. Time stood still until someone walking by broke the spell. "Should I buy it?" flashed through my mind, but I made myself turn away and walk out.

10

Spirit Bird

Soon after Mother's death, Bill's sister called to see how I was doing and to advise me to watch for the spirit bird that would signal to me that my mother was okay. She said it would appear in the next month and would be noticeable by doing something out of the ordinary. This was at the end of July, when our place seemed overrun with birds. Bluebirds and swallows, born in our special bluebird houses, were just fledging; colorful house and goldfinches came to the stream outside my study window to drink, then frequented our bird feeders. Hummingbirds zoomed in to eat at our hanging feeders. A Lazuli Bunting came occasionally to our pond to drink. A Killdeer we named Phoebe sat on eggs at the edge of our gravel driveway, protected only by the rock barrier we had built around her to keep cars away. A Great Blue Heron had started frequenting our pond at the beginning of the summer. With such an abundance of bird activity, I wasn't sure I would be able to distinguish which was the "spirit bird."

Waking to the sound of songbirds in the morning and hearing their twittering until dark gave Russ and me great pleasure. The birds were an important part of our lives. The only problem, despite his beauty, was the Great Blue Heron which had discovered the fish in our pond and acted as if they were his. The first time I saw the heron was in early June. I awoke one morning at daylight, opened my eyes to look out the window from where I lay in bed, and saw a giant bird perched on the top of a seventy-five foot hemlock. He stood, motionless and majestic, on the highest spire of the tree. It took a moment to register this sight and realize it wasn't part of a dream, and that the Great Blue Heron had come for breakfast. I nudged Russ. "Keep your eye on him," Russ cried as he swung out of bed, stuck his legs through his pants, and hobbled downstairs on stiff morning legs to scare him off before he gobbled another fish. The heron flew off when

Russ opened the door, but the vision of his silhouette against the early morning sky stayed with me. After that, I'd open my eyes every morning hoping to see him, a guilty pleasure since I knew he was there to catch our fish. His grace, elegance, and majesty thrilled me.

That spring, we had two large koi, named George and Mabel, and twelve smaller Sarassa and Shubunkin. By mid-summer, we had lost some of the small fish and knew if we didn't keep the heron away, he would eat them all. Russ consulted the internet to see what he could learn about protecting pond fish from herons. He found only sad stories about herons wiping out pond fish populations. Nobody had a good answer. We bought a device called a "Scarecrow" which attached to a hose and sprayed water over the pond when its electronic eye spotted movement. This didn't really bother the heron, but hearing the water spray alerted us to run outside and to scare him off.

Protecting the koi turned into an obsession for Russ who now woke before dawn and stood at the sliding door to the deck. When he caught a glimpse of the heron's wing movement in the trees or the bird's quiet stalking towards the pond, he went outside. We got used to hearing the Scarecrow go off between 4:30 and 6:00 in the morning. When it did, we both leapt out of bed. I'd go to the window to try to spot the heron while Russ would grab his pants and race downstairs. We performed this routine three to five times a week. The heron always left when it saw us, but came back later. We would catch him in the pond midmorning if we happened to be home.

The whole family knew about the heron and got to see it first hand during a winery board meeting at our house. We had started at 9:00, sitting in our living room, overlooking the deck that led to our koi pond. Halfway through the agenda, in the middle of discussing our five year strategic plan, I looked out and saw the heron standing in the pond. I jumped up, rushed to the sliding glass door and went out, followed by the others who finally had a chance to see what all the fuss was about. Bill, Nik, Alex, and Alison stood next to me on our deck watching as the great bird, less than twenty feet away, spread its wings and took off with a five inch Sarassa in its mouth, the bright orange fish clamped in the heron's long bill – a dramatic splash of color against the grey. Speechless with horror, but also with awe at what we had just witnessed, we all admitted to being secretly thrilled to see the heron perform so flawlessly what nature had equipped it to do.

Russ was out of town, having taken his mother on a two-week trip, so protecting the fish fell to me. I did the best I could. It was during this time that my mother went to the hospital three times, coming home only two. The night Russ came home I took a break from my vigil with my mother to be with him. Early the next morning, Russ went out to feed the fish and noticed that George, our large male koi, was in trouble. Russ donned his waders, went into the pond and discovered his prized fish had been speared. George was too big for the heron to take, but he had been mortally wounded. As I left for the hospital, Russ was preparing to put his favorite koi out of his misery. My mother and our prized fish died within hours of each other.

For the next month, we managed to keep the heron from consuming any more of our fish. We replaced George I with George II, who was even larger and, we hoped, too big for the heron to attempt. We ate dinner on the deck overlooking the pond every night and often saw the heron fly by.

One night in late August, we had a neighbor couple over. In the middle of dinner, the heron lit on one of the giant trees at the pond's edge. Noticing the movement and hearing the flutter of the giant wings, we all looked up to see the heron bathed in the glow of the setting sun, which cut a swath across the tree, highlighting him as a golden apparition against the greenery. He sat there, staying unusually long despite being aware of our presence. I had been sitting with my back to the pond so turned in my chair to see the glorious color and then went back to eating. "It's just our heron," Russ and I both replied and told heron stories as the bird flew off.

The next morning, just before breakfast, I was doing yoga on the living room floor when something swooshed by the window. I told Russ, who was in the kitchen. "It's the heron," he said, looking out. "He's at the top of one of the trees." Russ got the camera and took a few shots, recording for posterity the sight of such a big bird perched so perfectly at the top of a spindly branch of a very tall tree. I went out to get a better look and couldn't believe he was still there. Usually he flew off when he saw, or even heard us.

I looked up at this beautiful creature that had been tormenting us for the past two months. "Listen, you big gorgeous bird," I said. "You are so beautiful, so fabulous, so special." The heron didn't move and looked down at me like he was taking it all in. "Please stop going after our fish. We love our fish. Don't take them." The heron just kept looking at me while I spoke. When I stopped talking, he turned sideways and silently opened his beak very wide, forming a giant sideways V. Silent and motionless, he finally closed his beak, and looked down at me again, his eye locking on mine. Time seemed to stand still. Finally, he broke the connection, spread his great wings, and flew off. I felt a chill go up my spine. I had no trouble recognizing my mother's spirit bird. I think he had come the night before while we were having dinner to deliver his message, but we were busy with guests. He returned the next morning to try again; my mother was safe and our fish would be safe too. Indeed, it was more than a year before we saw another heron at our pond. By that time our little fish had multiplied to the point that we welcomed him back to thin the pack.

The symbolism of the heron as my mother's messenger was perfect. Two charismatic, elegant creatures who aroused conflicting emotions, nourishing one part of me and treading on another. The heron represented closure, a letting go of what had kept mother and me apart. That was a first step. It would be years before I accepted how much of my mother was inside me.

The ceremonial passing of the Baton, January 2nd, 2008.
L to R: Me (holding the "Administrative Tool"), Alex, Alison, Bill.

L to R: Alex, Alison, and Nik in front of young Pinot Noir vines, 2005.

Bill Blosser wearing his favorite French beret, holding baby Pinot Noir grapevines we were about to plant, 1971.

When we opened our tasting room, I poured wine for customers on weekends. This photo shows our early wine label. Behind me on the wall is a framed needlepoint my mother did for me. Underneath that are our first medals for our wines, 1978.

In 1980 I started managing the vineyard and was in the field on a daily basis. The tractor was my workhorse. Note that the hillside in the background shows open fields. By the late 1980s, what had been wheat and hay had become vineyard, as Domaine Drouhin of Oregon planted the hillside and built a winery, 1982.

First generation: Bill and I check building plans during the construction of Sokol Blosser Winery's tasting room. Four year old Alex, in his Big Bird shirt, and our dog Muffin were with us, 1978.

The next generation: Co-presidents, Alison and Alex, consult plans during construction of the winery's new tasting room. Alison's dog, Twix, is with them, 2013.

Designed by John Storrs, a noted Portland architect at the time, our first tasting room was built in 1978. Originally open only on weekends, by the late 1980s, there was enough demand to be open seven days a week. With one moderately large room, a tiny kitchen and office, it seemed to grow smaller and smaller as more and more visitors came to Oregon wine country.

Second Generation. Designed by Brad Cloepfil and built in 2013, the wood and glass building seemed to rise out of the vineyard. With a catering kitchen, a library for special tastings, a large deck, and spaces for private events, it set a benchmark for Oregon wine hospitality. Photo by Andréa Johnson, 2013.

As winemaker, Russ participated in major vineyard decisions, especially when to harvest. He and I regularly walked the vineyard to check out the grapes, 2000.

Russ's office served as tasting headquarters — the place where key blending decisions were made. Here Alex, Russ, and I are tasting samples drawn from barrels of Pinot Noir. Since each block of Pinot Noir was picked, vinified, and barreled separately, we had 60-80 different lots to taste, 2004.

My father, Gus Sokol. This formal photo of my father in his 70's, (before the Alzheimer's) was taken in our family home in Milwaukee, WI. The leather chair, his stylish suit and shirt, the bust of George Bernard Shaw, and the shelves of leather covered books, combine to capture the man. All that's missing is a glass of wine.

Dora Bederov Richter,
the matriarch and great
grandmother I never knew but
who loomed large through
my mother's stories.
She emigrated from
Odessa, Russia about 1890,
in her mid-twenties, the same age
I was when we started
our vineyard.

My mother, Phyllis Sokol, on the left and me on the right,
both photos taken at age 21. I fought for years the idea that we looked
so much alike. These pictures erase any doubt.

Publicity photo of the all-woman band, my mother organized and led during the late 1920s. My mother is in the center, on the left side of the piano, 1928.

Spirit Bird. The Great Blue Heron that frequented our little pond, perched on top of a 75 foot evergreen tree.

Three generations. I had to travel to Chicago for a wine event.
I took Alison for the experience and my mother to see her old haunts as she was born and raised in Chicago. Here we are: Alison, aged 15, sporting her teenage braces; my mother, Phyllis Sokol, a spritely 89, and me, aged 50, 1994.

What a sense of passing time:
Alison Sokol Blosser, Co-President of Sokol Blosser Winery, with the former President, her mother, me, 2013.

Russ and I in the barrel cellar, 2002.
Russ is using a glass instrument called a wine thief to extract wine for tasting out of the barrel.

Alex and I in the Watershed Block, the highest point of our estate vineyard. Andre, Alex's faithful dog, always by his side. Andre was famous among the staff for his lightening ability to grab food off the table. Photo by Doreen L. Wynja, 2005.

Zasu and I stopping on our daily walk up the winery road, 2010.

Alison, with the smile of victory at completing her first half triathlon, 2010.

Alison, dazzling on her wedding day, 2012. Photo courtesy Angela Smith.

The New Leaders: Alex, Alison, and Nik in the late autumn vineyard. Alison had just had her second baby, Luca, and came back to be in the photo, 2013.

Held at the peak of harvest season, the Bounty of Yamhill County (BOYC), was designed to showcase the area's splendid chefs, family farms, and famous wines. What could be better than a farm-to-table meal in a vineyard setting, accompanied by great wine and conversation, 2014. Photo courtesy of Andréa Johnson.

Nik and I at Bounty of Yamhill County's Big Night dinner at Sokol Blosser Winery. Photo courtesy of Andréa Johnson, 2012.

How to address the several hundred guests at
BOYC's Big Night dinner? We had no stage or podium, so Russ got
a ladder from the winery and held it while I climbed up to
welcome people and thank the sponsors, 2014.
Photo courtesy of Andréa Johnson.

11

Wedding

Many of the winery staff admitted to being afraid of Russ, and I could see why. He cultivated a stern demeanor, a veneer to protect his vulnerability. I could relate to that, since I also had a protective shell. But as he let me into his world, Russ's playful side came out. One day, as we turned into a gas station to fill up on our way home from the beach, Russ pointed to the large RV ahead of us and turned to me without warning: "God dammit Mabel! Isn't that Fred and Babs from back home in Iowa? That's got to be him. I can't believe there's more than one guy who wears those ridiculous chartreuse pants. Jesus Christ, duck down, Mabel. We don't want him to see us."

I looked around to make sure there was no one else in the car he could be talking to, then got it and responded, "Listen, George, you just stop being so hard on folks. You aren't any fashion plate yourself. We've got another hour of driving before we get to the exhibit of the world's biggest ball of string and I want to get going so we have lots of time before it closes. Are you still hungry? We have one Twinkie left."

Once we started our version of Archie and Edith Bunker – our George and Mabel repartee – it would surface unexpectedly with verbal banter, usually when we were driving in the car, and always with "God dammit, Mabel...." It spilled over into emails and phone messages when I was traveling. One of us would start and the other would respond in character. Call it arrogant, politically incorrect, or just plain stupid, we both found the silliness of our alternative personas a relief valve – an unexpected outlet for the wackiness each of us stored inside, hidden behind our rather staid façades.

Russ and I had already lived together for almost seven years, devoted to each other, but neither feeling the need to formalize the relationship. We talked about marriage occasionally and always agreed it wasn't necessary. When people asked why we didn't get married, I usually replied we had more fun living in sin. Since we bought a house to live together in 1999, then built at the vineyard in 2006, we felt we had made a significant enough commitment.

After we became a couple, I continued to introduce Russ as our winemaker, leaving people to wonder about our relationship. "Spousal equivalent" or "boyfriend," seemed silly, so I just left it at winemaker. We would do events at the winery where we would be all business, with no hint of personal relationship, then leave together to walk down the hill to our house, holding hands.

Then, while I was struggling through the final year of the transition, the idea of making a formal commitment suddenly seemed right. I'm not sure what triggered the switch in my thinking, but one wintry Sunday, in January 2007, we sat in our living room, each with a cat on our lap, watching the juncos and finches flock to our bird feeders, and an NFL football game on TV. On impulse, I turned to Russ.

"I've been thinking about marriage," I told him. He looked at me quizzically.

"Anyone in particular?"

"How about you and me?" I said. I was smiling but he could see I was serious. His tone changed.

"Why, after all these years, are you thinking about marriage? We're committed to each other. Do we need a formal piece of paper to prove it?"

"It just feels like it's time," I said.

"Okay," Russ said. "I guess it is."

Wanting to marry Russ and start again as a wife, signified a letting go of my past. I didn't realize how much I had held on to the memory until I let it go. I could not have made a new commitment without that final disengagement.

I imagined a casual wedding. I'd wear a turtleneck and a fleece vest, not a wedding dress. We'd go to a Justice of the Peace. Although he acted like he was just going along, Russ made the first public announcement by leaning over at a formal wine industry dinner and whispering to Alison that he and I were going to get married. His announcement stopped her mid-sentence and she immediately wanted details. When Russ told her what we were thinking of doing, she said, "Don't even think you can get married without us," making it clear that she and her brothers would want to be involved. "You can even go to Hawaii if you want," she said, hinting at what she thought we should do. "You just have to take us with you."

No one was going to control my wedding this time. I put wedding plans on hold to let the idea of family involvement sink in. Hawaii was out of the question, but getting married at the vineyard would work and certainly be appropriate for us. So we decided to make it more public, although running off alone and quietly getting married would have avoided all the little decisions that a staged event involved.

I tackled the details one by one. John Collins, an attorney friend whom I hadn't seen for years and had became a judge, agreed to perform the ceremony. I scoured ***The New Yorker*** website and found a 1925 cover, a drawing of a couple entwined on a park bench, that made a perfect wedding invitation. Alison helped me search Portland to find the right outfit, a flowing Eileen Fisher ensemble.

Alex asked who I wanted to "give me away." His suggestion hit a hot button. Nobody was going to "give" me away. If he and Nik had wanted to escort me, I cut them off with my fierce independent stance. I had fought hard to become my own person and wanted to walk by myself. In hindsight, I regret that stance; it would have been lovely to walk on the arms of my two adult sons.

I thought of a more acceptable option that would include males of the family and asked if Alex's twin boys, Avery and Nikolas, would walk with me. These two spirited five year olds had three modes of getting from here to there: running, skipping, or jumping. We practiced walking slowly and deliberately, with their staying next to me, not getting ahead. "Your job is to get the three of us to Russ, all at the same time," I told them at the end of our practice. They looked at me solemnly before scampering off.

I put a lot more thought into getting married at sixty-two than I had at twenty-one. This ceremony would be our pledge to each other, a public statement, witnessed by friends and family. I wondered if marriage would change us. I had known couples who had lived together for years, then broken up after they got married.

On September 9th, 2007, we became husband and wife in a simple morning ceremony outside on the winery's paved crush pad overlooking the vineyard, attended by only immediate family, a few close friends and employees. Bill was out of town and couldn't attend, but his mother and sister did. His mother sat next to Russ's mom. As I walked up the aisle, escorted by two serious little boys in white shirts and bow ties, I smiled to myself seeing the two smallish white-haired women sitting together, both unusually caring and supportive mothers-in-law.

My first marriage service had been a traditional Episcopal ceremony with vows coming straight from the book. Here was my chance to put the partnership I wanted into words. I wanted to convey what getting married now meant to me. Since I had so much trouble being myself in my relationship with Bill, I wanted to be explicit in my relationship with Russ that we were two individuals coming together. We used the imagery of two candles whose flames come together to make a brighter light even though they remain separate candles, then captured the essence of the right relationship in this vow that was part of the ceremony:

"It is not your responsibility to make the other person happy. But the quality of your presence and partnership with the other person will have a lot to do with the happiness that abides in your home. A successful marriage is not a miraculous gift. It is rather a human achievement. Happiness through marriage has something of a mystic quality about it. There are no universal rules, but we know that life through marriage can be made radiant."

We looked at each other as Judge Collins read this. Oblivious to anything but each other, both of us had misty eyes when we repeated our vows. The balmy morning, the picturesque vineyard, the smiling upturned faces of family and friends, are engraved in my memory.

Our friend Heidi had offered to sing for us. I had known Heidi for fifteen years and considered her a close friend. We regularly spent time together. Yet her offer surprised me. I knew her as a writer and journalist, had never heard her sing, and had no knowledge of her musical talent. She chose the Beatles song, "In My Life," a love song for adults, acknowledging past loves while cherishing the present. Her clear, lilting soprano floated out over the Pinot Noir vines ripening in the September sun.

The whole ceremony took a scant fifteen minutes. Afterwards, we hosted a celebratory brunch in the vineyard. Russ and I sat in the middle of a giant U-shaped table, against the backdrop of the vines. Sprays of purple, rosy, and yellow flowers, entwined with the green of our grapevines, ran down the center of the tables, which overflowed with platters of wild Chinook salmon, roasted summer vegetables, ripe heirloom tomatoes with fresh mozzarella, watermelon-berry salad, and wine glasses of sparkling wine and Pinot Noir. Our guests took turns toasting.

Saying our vows in front of friends and family struck something deep inside and gave me increased respect for the marriage ritual and public statement of commitment. When we turned in that night, we agreed it had been a glorious day.

12

Transition Ends

As we entered the last quarter of the practice year, it was clear the transition wasn't over for me yet. My impulse to control continued erupting. When I saw problems in the vineyard, I made sure Alex knew about it. But when I told him, I felt the wall between us. His defensiveness unnerved me.

We arranged for Alex, Alison, and me to meet with Marsia as referee. In the safety of her office, Alex's suppressed feelings flowed out. He admitted he didn't like my questioning him. He felt I had made some bad decisions in the past, like embracing biodynamic farming and listening to consultants. When I was knocked off the pedestal he had me on, he went from thinking I could do no wrong to thinking everything I did was wrong. Now he was the decision maker and didn't want me interfering.

I didn't see it as interfering. Many vineyard decisions are judgment calls, worthy of discussion of the pros and cons, like when to harvest, taking into account the grapes' ripeness, the current weather, the forecasted weather, and what other blocks of grapes are due to come in. My experience could be helpful; I wanted to be consulted. I wondered if we would ever reach a point where I could ask, and Alex would feel unthreatened enough, to engage in a discussion.

My strained relations with Alex showed me another part of the transition I would need to resolve – changing my relationship with Alex and Alison from boss back to Mom, from supervision to support. Marsia laid it on the line for me later: "Do you love your son enough to have the strength to let him go? Are you able to stand back and let him bear the burden of his decisions?" This view had not occurred to me, yet I knew exactly what she meant. "He's trying to individuate, to figure out who he really is," she told me. "If you try to bear the pain of this process for him, you'll smother him. The more you can let go, the better off he'll be in the rest of his life. You've got to trust that he'll come through," she finished.

Alex and I had worked closely for the last eight years with me as chief. I thought I had surrendered the leadership role, but clearly had not. In trying to prevent Alex from making the wrong decision, I unwittingly kept him in the role of a child, alienating him because, to his credit, he didn't want the child's role.

My mother had tried to control me emotionally. I was horrified to learn I was doing a similar thing to my son. It had taken me many years to confront my childhood issues. Alex might come through or he might not, but I needed to stay out of it and leave him alone to work it out. The force of my love needed to be redirected, from protection to release.

I would never again equate "letting go" as a sign of weakness. This would take a strength I wasn't sure I had. From then on, I kept my distance from Alex, the only way not to interfere. I missed him, and a long period of cordial estrangement ensued. Except for winery board meetings, our interaction for the next four years revolved around family times, like being Grandma to his boys. He told me later he appreciated the distance and felt the love it took to do it.

Towards the end of the final year of transition, just when I started to think how well I was doing, something came along to slap me on the side of the head and let me know how much farther I had to go: the word "retirement" was my next nemesis. The first public announcement of my stepping back came out in my President's letter for the winery's October wine club shipment. Our Cellar Club comprised our best and most loyal customers. I wrote in the newsletter that we would be announcing a big change after the first of the year: on January 2, 2008, I would be stepping down. Alex and Alison would take over as co-presidents of the winery. I would still be around, but they would be in charge. After writing the letter in September, I forgot about it.

The good news was that our members read my letter. That became evident during the winery's Thanksgiving Open House, when Cellar Club members came up to me smiling. "Congratulations. How does it feel to be retired?" they'd ask. Every time I heard "retired," I shuddered, hoping they didn't see the look of fear in my eyes. I managed to laugh and say I'd talked Alison and Alex into doing my work for me, but the involuntary cringe when I heard the "**R**" word told me

I was still vulnerable.

Little more than a month later, the practice year was over. After three years, I was finally ready. I may not have looked any different but when we "flipped the switch" I felt as if a great weight had been taken off my shoulders. I had no idea what the future held. But finally I was ready to ask, "What's next?" All I knew was that "next" would not be at Sokol Blosser Winery.

As the co-presidents took control of the winery, in 2008, the economy was booming. They had big plans for expansion and talked excitedly about producing new wines and expanding markets. Within six months Lehman Brothers failed, the largest bankruptcy in United States history which, combined with a mortgage crisis and general bank overextension, set off a major recession. Restaurant business fell precipitously. Wine sales plummeted. Alex and Alison shelved their expansion plans and hit the streets to bolster wine sales. Selling current inventory became top priority.

They were learning how precarious a business could be, a lesson Bill and I had learned over and over. I assumed they'd come to me for advice and felt slighted when they didn't. When I came to the winery, Alex would look up, say "Hi Mom," then put his head down and go back to work. Alison was always on the phone or concentrating on her computer. They were obviously working hard, but I had to wonder if their reluctance to engage meant they were afraid I might try to take over or give them unasked for advice.

Even though I occasionally represented the winery, the winery camaraderie no longer included me. When friends and acquaintances came to me for donations or requests for winery involvement, I directed them to the new decision makers. Removed from the winery's daily swirl, I had little reason to go to my office there. I began to check my winery voicemail from home; my winery office sat empty.

The practice year had taken its toll. I felt pummeled, physically and emotionally. It was as if the universe, trying to teach me the importance of learning to let go, was impelled to deliver the message in as many ways possible. During that final transition year, the marquee event was letting go of my identity as President of Sokol Blosser. But letting go of my mother, my first marriage, and Alex, added depth, texture and complexity.

Giving up the winery had left a big void. I had been important and now wasn't. I needed to reinvent my life, but felt the need to reintegrate the parts of myself that my public persona had shoved out of the way for so many years. Pat Frishkoff's first concern – what will Mom do – was still the relevant question and I was finally ready to acknowledge it.

The vines in the vineyard turn inward after giving up their fruit at harvest, sending all remaining energy down to their roots. We see them as dormant, but their physical appearance masks their internal activity as they prepare for the next cycle. It struck me that, like the vines, I needed to turn inward to renew.

13

Inward

As a college student in the 1960s, I found my niche with other serious students. We saw ourselves as highbrow and intellectual although, looking back, I suspect we were more likely humorless and arrogant. We made fun of fraternity parties as mindless drinking orgies, and the football rallies and bonfires as shallow and materialistic. My freshman year, when I attended a fraternity party, my stereotypes were reinforced. When I entered the stately white stucco frat house with some of my dorm mates, I was immediately handed a plastic cup with a drink that looked like lemonade. It was fruit punch so liberally laced with gin or vodka that it took less than one glass for me to understand why they called it a Velvet Hammer. Everyone else at the party looked giddy and happy; I just felt nauseated and dizzy. I stumbled out, getting as far as the front lawn before falling to my knees and vomiting. Ashamed, humiliated, embarrassed, and still nauseous, I somehow made my way back to my dorm, having learned about both fraternity parties and my minimal capacity for alcohol. I had no inkling that my life would revolve around wine. My low alcohol tolerance later became an asset, helping me avoid the threat of alcoholism, an occupational hazard of the wine industry.

But college was for experimentation. My parents were 3000 miles away and I was free to choose. I just had to figure out what the right choices were. Students at fraternity parties didn't seem to be asking the questions that interested me. I gravitated to others who were and spent many evenings with other earnest students, sitting around a candlelit table at a student apartment or professor's home. We weren't drinking. Wine bottles on the table dripped wax, not wine. As the candles burned down to stubs, we sparred in heated discussions about the meaning of life and the nature of man. Were humans naturally violent? Was war inevitable? With sober intensity, we quoted Ayn Rand, Plato,

Nietzsche, Camus, even Jesus, trying to find answers. The discussions were stimulating but inconclusive, our questions left hanging, unresolved.

Those conversations ended when I left academic life. The quest stayed in abeyance, like pressing a pause button for the next forty years. Having babies, raising children, starting a vineyard and winery, focusing on business – just holding it together – took up all my time and energy. When the daily pressures of running a business and fronting a presidential persona evaporated, the gnarly questions of life resurfaced.

As I started my inner journey, I thought about my ecumenical upbringing. My heritage was Jewish. Both parents came from observant Jewish families. Mother had been active in a Jewish sorority in college. When we started the winery, Daddy told me that his grandfather had made wine for his synagogue in Brooklyn. But when they married, in 1930, my mother, aged twenty-five, and father, aged thirty-one, made a conscious decision to turn away from Judaism, not to raise their children as Jews. I wasn't raised in a Jewish household, felt no connection to that heritage, and was a teenager before I even learned of it. Judaism was so unfamiliar that, as an adult, when invited to a Seder (ceremonial dinner for the beginning of Passover), I had to ask what it was.

I didn't ask my mother about her decision until after my father had died, so his version stays mute. She didn't remember it as difficult and voiced no regrets. She told me others in her family did the same, one cousin even changing his family name from Feingold to Field. My brother, Ronnie, and I have since discussed their decision at length, concluding that during an era of intense anti-Semitism, our parents, like many other Jews at the time, sought to disengage from a religion that no longer spoke to them and had dangerous consequences.

Mother sought a new religious connection. She attended various churches, starting with Christian Science, then worked her way up more rigorous Christian sects, spending the last forty years of her life as a devoted Episcopalian. I reflected her journey and was baptized Congregational, confirmed Methodist, and married in the Episcopal Church. Daddy had no pull towards any church. It took a wedding or a funeral to get him inside one. In high school I asked him if he believed in God. He responded that he believed in a "life force." I wondered what a life force looked like. I knew what God and Jesus looked like since Sunday school walls were covered with pictures of them.

Bill had attended the Episcopal Church as a child and grown away as he grew up. When he and I raised our children, the extent of their religious training was following both our families' tradition of saying grace before holiday meals. The children participated. Ten-year-old Alex's grace one Thanksgiving, "Please let the pies be good," became an annual family refrain.

My Christian world had allowed only minor infringement. The first breach came in 1961, my summer as an exchange student in Tokyo, living with Sachiko and her family. I felt like I had entered a different world. My height and fair complexion created quite a stir at their home in one of the oldest parts of the city where few Japanese had seen Westerners. When Sachiko and her older sister and I walked through the narrow bustling streets in their neighborhood, past tiny roll-up-door shops, people stopped what they were doing and stared outright. Not only was I fair skinned and blue-eyed, I was almost a head taller than they.

I was as interested in them as they were in me. Everything was new to me, especially the food. Not only what to eat, but how to eat it. In 1961, sushi was not the ubiquitous American food it is today. Maneuvering chopsticks, eating raw fish with seaweed and boiled rice with every meal, including breakfast, represented a radical departure from my Wisconsin meat and potatoes palate. Difficulty controlling my chopsticks didn't stop me from eating. I went home twelve pounds heavier, barely able to button my clothes, a condition my brothers immediately pointed out.

One evening, at the end of dinner, my Japanese mother smiled encouragingly as Sachiko explained, in halting English, that the spirits of their dead ancestors would return that night. My first impulse was to laugh as images of kimono-clad spirits floating in the dark flashed through my mind. I knew Japan would be different, but this was too weird. My Japanese family, however, wasn't laughing. This solemn ritual occurred once a year. My Japanese mother assigned tasks to each of the five children to make sure the spirits could get in and find food. This was the one of many Japanese customs which challenged my western sensibilities.

Over the summer we visited so many Buddhist shrines and temples, I lost count. But I never forgot my reaction the night the spirits of family ancestors returned. It took something unimaginable in my world – like dead people visiting – to make me take notice. Forty-six years later I circled back, ready at last to break out of my western mindset. When I finally approached Buddhism, as part of my inner journey, the shell that had started to splinter while I was in Japan, cracked wide open.

Reincarnation, selflessness, being in the moment. These stretched me like mental spandex. In college, History of Western Civilization had been a required course. Studying the rest of the world was optional. Western thought emphasized the importance of self, personal achievement, ego development, mind over matter. "I think, therefore I am." I understood and lived that tradition. Being president of a business exemplified its archetype. Heaven or Hell, as reward or punishment for performance, established the course of Christian capitalists in America, starting with the Mayflower pilgrims.

The idea that there was something beyond the ego, a soul that, like all energy, could change form but not be eliminated, intrigued me. As I thought about reincarnation and selflessness, it occurred to me that I had no problem accepting the cycle of dissolution and rebirth in the vineyard and, indeed, in all of nature. So why wouldn't that include humans too? Maybe there was a world beyond the particulars of everyday life, beyond the dimension where I lived.

Maybe my father was on to something when he talked about a life force. If energy is eternal and only changes shape and form, maybe there is an energetic force, a "through line," that moves through families. What we call the science of genetics could just as well be soul energy that is reincarnated in family lines.

My friend Heidi, knowing my quest, invited me to go with her to a Buddhist retreat center for a three day silent retreat. I'd never been to a Buddhist retreat center, or on a silent retreat, or done any meditation. It would all be new, but that was what I was after. Not speaking for three days was a little intimidating but I reasoned that if my talkative friend Heidi could be silent for three days, I could too.

Off we went, on a rainy November day, leaving behind cell phones, computers, even reading material. Nothing that might distract us from going inward was allowed. For three days, I was one of forty women who sat in silence and focused on Metta, the Pali word for Lovingkindness. The teacher led us at first, repeating phrases wishing love, health, forgiveness, and acceptance. She instructed us to aim these good wishes initially at ourselves, not others. We had to learn to love ourselves before we could love others. I thought I needed to love others first. If they loved me back, then I could love myself. Maybe I had it backwards all these years.

I found repeating the Metta phrases for my children and Russ comforting. But trying to say them for myself triggered angst, even tears. I simply couldn't wish myself well-being and happiness. The Metta experience showed me that something lay deep inside that needed to be brought to light, understood, and treated with compassion. That process would take years, but a little light had been let in. Sitting in companionable silence with forty strangers and learning Metta affected me profoundly. I felt like an old duck discovering a pond for the first time, giddy with wonder and delight at this new find which turned out to be a basic necessity.

Another unexpected teacher on my inner journey turned out to be a dog. At the end of the business transition, while musing over what to do with my newfound time, I mentioned that it might be fun to get a puppy. Tired of being serious all the time, I thought a cuddly, frolicsome puppy might help me be more playful. The idea, simply a passing thought, might have died but for Alison actively promoting it. She presented me with a book at Christmas describing various dog breeds and their features. Her big white standard poodle had been a source of comfort and companionship to her. She thought a dog might do the same for me.

We always had at least one dog in the house while I was growing up. Then two mixed breeds, Muffin and Bagel, were my pals in the vineyard. I had fond memories of those days and could see myself with a dog companion again. I loved Alison's dog and remembered my mother's sweet-tempered standard poodle when I was in high school. Poodles were smart and didn't shed, so we wouldn't be fighting dog hair in the house, a key factor for my less than enthusiastic husband.

Russ finally agreed, against his better judgment as he repeatedly reminded me later. I was willing to splurge and pay for a poodle puppy, so Alison, who had been waiting for the signal, contacted her dog's breeder. With lightening speed, my efficient daughter arranged to drive Russ and me to visit her breeder, just to "look" at the puppies. Of course they were irresistible. Soon we were driving home with me cradling an armful of black fluff, trying to think of a name and wondering what lay ahead. Russ came up with the name, Zasu, taken from a favorite CD of French cafe music.

I started a puppy obedience class but immediately ran into trouble. Zasu acted unusually fearful and reactive both to other dogs and to people. All my books advised exposing my puppy to new experiences – taking her where there were people and noise, Home Depot for example. But Zasu pulled away from people and froze with fear at noise. She was constantly on what Russ called "high alert" barking frantically at things that scared her, which seemed to be everything. At home in the evenings, she'd bark uncontrollably at the sliding door at something we couldn't see or hear. When we took her for a walk she lunged at every car that went by. If she happened to be off leash outside and saw a car go up the winery road, she chased after it.

"This can't go on like this. I can't take it," Russ said. I stopped counting the times he said he was sorry he had let me talk him into getting a puppy and should have listened to his gut that told him not to do it. Tension between us began to build over the dog. Since I had brought the dog into the house, her bad behavior was somehow my fault. I felt guilty at imposing my will on Russ, guilty at my failure to control my puppy, and sad to the point of despair. I defended her, but this was not the cuddly puppy I had envisioned.

On the plus side, she ate well, house-trained easily, and enchanted us as she ran like a gazelle through the vineyard. She slept in a crate next to my side of the bed. She was most affectionate in the morning when, still half asleep, she stretched out as I stroked her, luxuriating in the moment. I liked her puppy smell and would crawl halfway into her crate to massage her and inhale the sweet scent of her fur. But when I tried to pet her during the day, she stiffened. I thought having a dog would help me learn to relax and play, but this was turning out to be hugely stressful; I began to think getting a dog was a big mistake. Everybody I told had advice and a dog story to tell. One acquaintance told me her poodle had been so unmanageable she had sent him to a month-long "boot camp" where he was trained with an electric collar; he came back well-behaved. I looked at my little puppy that was so scared of the world and thought a shock collar would destroy her. There had to be another way.

I enrolled Zasu at a doggy day care so she could play with other dogs, and I could have a break. She seemed eager to be there and jumped around wildly with anticipation every time we went in the door. Then one day, minutes before I was to deliver a keynote address at a conference in downtown Portland, the owner of the daycare called to tell me Zasu had nipped one of the handlers when the handler got between Zasu and another dog; Zasu was no longer welcome at their facility. Please come get her.

Here I was, in downtown Portland, about to deliver a speech to several hundred people. I walked up to the podium holding myself under tight control until I was finished and could go outside, get in the car, and let down. The daycare owner later decided it wasn't as serious a situation as they had initially thought. Zasu was forgiven and allowed to return. But the episode unnerved me. I called the breeder, who surprised me with her advice: "Put the dog down and get another puppy." Her coldhearted response horrified me, conveying a new perspective on such breeders. For her, dogs were a commodity; if they didn't work out, she discarded them.

The owner of the doggy day care suggested that an animal communicator, might help me understand Zasu better. Here was a profession I'd never heard of. I was surprised that someone actually made a living talking to animals. I remembered the Dr. Doolittle books of my childhood, but he was imaginary. We met at the doggy daycare office. I expected a person who dealt in other dimensions to float out in something gauzy, maybe a mauve caftan and feather earrings, so I was surprised when Lauren appeared, looking and talking like an ordinary person, wearing pressed jeans and a crisp cotton shirt. Her no-nonsense demeanor destroyed my stereotype.

Before starting to work with Zasu, Lauren explained that she wouldn't be talking to the puppy in the room, but rather to Zasu's "higher self." I had to take a minute to let that sink in. It hadn't occurred to me that Zasu had a higher self, but why not? If I had a soul, a self that came back in many guises, why wouldn't Zasu, or any other animal for that matter? I was ready to quiet my western bias and my need for visible proof. The message from the heron as my mother's spirit bird had opened me to the possibility of communication between animals and humans.

While Lauren communicated with Zasu's higher self, the physical Zasu played on the floor, oblivious to what was going on. The room was silent except for the sound of Zasu's nails scratching the linoleum floor as she played with a ball. Lauren reported that Zasu liked dogs better than people and didn't want to have to be social with humans. She particularly didn't want to be a winery ambassador like Alison's dog. I had been taking Zasu to the winery, trying to socialize her, never considering that she might not want the role Alison's friendly dog seemed to love. I had approached Zasu with certain expectations, one of which was that she would be more extroverted. Yet I didn't like being with crowds of people; I liked to control the situation; I had difficulty letting my soft, affectionate side surface. Zasu seemed like my mirror image, as if she were me in dog form.

I realized I was trying to change Zasu into the dog I wanted, rather than letting her be the personality she was. I wasn't sure where the line lay between training and individuality. Russ continued to blame me for introducing bedlam since our lives revolved around dealing with her barking, her fear of people, and her stalking and harassing our cat.

We couldn't take Zasu in public or even have friends or family over without stressing over how she would act. I found myself holding on to a dog who was alienating everyone around me. After nine months, I gave up and finally admitted that Zasu was too difficult for me to manage. Accepting failure did not come easily, but I finally faced my defeat, as well as how unhappy I had made my husband.

I would find Zasu a home where she would be happy. Alison, who felt responsible for encouraging me to get a puppy, took over and called a poodle rescue group for me. She, and all the people who had worked with Zasu, tried to help me find her another home. Three times we had someone ready to take her. Each time it fell through. After the third time, I stopped trying to re-home her. Zasu apparently was meant to stay with us.

This led me to reflect on why Zasu was in my life. The conventional, practical side of me argued she was just a dog, a dog with problems. If they were too difficult, I should get rid of her. The breeder who advised me to put her down represented this extreme. My newly attuned metaphysical side sensed there was a reason we were together. She may not have been the dog I envisioned, but she was the dog I had. My challenge was to figure out what I needed to learn from her and vice-versa. Animal communication had taught me how much of a two way street this was—not only did Zasu have something to teach me, but she had chosen me to help her on her evolutionary path. I needed to keep working with her to discover why we were together.

While I pondered all this, Lauren told me about a friend of hers a few hours away in Washington State, a "poodle person" who did water therapy and training for dogs. I hoped she could do for Zasu what none of our previous efforts had accomplished. Russ was willing to try. He thought this might be our last chance. We arranged to leave Zasu there while we went to Hawaii for a much needed vacation. This was the start of the turnaround, although it would take another year of learning before I felt comfortable managing Zasu.

Beth, the trainer, first trained Zasu, then trained me—an equally daunting task, since I was convinced I had failed. Beth managed Zasu with confidence. I had less fear speaking before an audience of 500 people than handling this dog. Her instructions were clear and unequivocal – use a harness, a collar, and a leash with two points of contact. But don't restrain her. "Loose leash is the key in getting Zasu to exert self-control," she said. "If she wants to lunge or pull, give her a tug, then loosen the leash immediately. If you hold her back, she will automatically pull against you. If you give her room, she will balance herself." This was counterintuitive for me and so metaphorical—letting go to attain self-control.

Zasu's behavior improved as I learned how to handle her, but she still had more to teach me. Her continued nervousness at any sound or movement worried me. Lauren suggested I take Zasu to another friend of hers who did energy healing work. She thought maybe this would help Zasu calm down and be more at peace in her body. I didn't understand what energy healing entailed, but Lauren's credibility was high since she had led me to Beth. Maybe what Zasu needed was metaphysical. Maybe she was on the same journey I was. I made an appointment with Lauren's friend, Sheila, for an energy healing session.

Sheila lived in a retirement community of neatly appointed mobile homes, but hers stood out by the lushness of her flower garden. I asked her what made these plants so happy. Was it enriched soil or special fertilizer? "No," Sheila said. "It's Reiki. I do Reiki on my garden." I was beginning to think everything could be reduced to energy flow.

We went into her treatment room and sat on the floor. Sheila started moving her hands around Zasu, about a foot from her body. I waited for Zasu to react. To my surprise, she didn't seem to mind. She lay down and stretched out. Sheila's hands moved silently up and down, back and forth, as if she were playing the harp while doing Tai Chi. I had no idea what she was doing but didn't want to break the silence or her concentration by asking. So I sat and watched with amazement as Zasu gradually relaxed. At one point my high-strung dog took a deep breath and the tension in her furry body seemed to visibly drain away.

"I think it's hard to be Zasu," Sheila told me when she finally stopped. I appreciated that she was looking at the world from Zasu's point of view. She said she detected gaps in Zasu's energy field near her hind quarters and felt that Zasu's higher self was not fully integrated into her earthly body. We went back three more times for energy treatments. Each time Zasu lay down and let herself relax in a way I hadn't seen at home. Each time I watched, amazed.

Looking back at the bumpy, painful path on which Zasu led me, I realize how much I learned from her. It took her extreme behavior to lead me to animal communication and energy healing. These practices were beyond my imagination only one year earlier. Friends and family couldn't understand why I kept this dog and rolled their eyes when I told them about these oddball practices. I did a lot, probably more than most, but Zasu was an important part of my inner journey. Her gift was to show me that I could either admit defeat or open to new experiences. My gift to her was not to give up until I helped her. My puppy did not turn out to be my anticipated playmate, but she had another role. She took me into realms I wouldn't have entered without her. I would never again think of my animal companions as "just a dog," or "just a cat." Zasu was another being, here on her own journey.

Russ's complaining about her made me so defensive that at one point I wondered if I would have to make a choice between them. I was so involved with Zasu, I wasn't sure who it would be. Then, slowly, Zasu won Russ over. Summer evenings, Russ took Zasu outside and threw a Frisbee for her. I think Russ was taken in by her grace and agility. She would leap in the air to catch it and bring it back to him to throw again.This became their time together. Mornings, when Russ left for work, Zasu jumped on the couch to look out the window, barking plaintively as she watched him walk up the hill to the winery.

14

Inner/Outer

I spent almost two years studying, learning meditation, trying to discover the self that dwelled inside my public persona. Spending much of my time alone at home with Zasu, it was a stark contrast to my life of the previous seventeen years. My silk suits gathered dust in the closet, while my jeans, turtlenecks, and fleece vests frayed with use. I had let a part of me die, giving up my position at the winery; I could feel myself starting to grow again. The continuous arising and dissolving life cycle of the vineyard had a deeper meaning now.

It seemed to me that Buddhist dharma, animal communication, organic agriculture, and biodynamic farming all gave the same message: we live in an energetic universe of constant change. All life is composed of energy which can neither be created nor destroyed, only redirected. Everything I studied on my inner journey ultimately spoke as one voice, with a cosmic spaciousness that put my life and my world of everyday stresses in the temporal perspective of being a dot on a continuous timeline. Energy flowed across lifetimes, across species, across the cosmos. Each field of study had its unique perspective and recommended path, but they all led to the same place, the interweaving of life across time and space.

How my inner journey fit into the practical side of my life wasn't yet clear. There was no burning bush, but I understood that part of my mission now was to use what I had learned to go forward. I didn't want to retreat to an ashram, but rather use this sensitivity to move forward. While I no longer ran Sokol Blosser Winery, I remained part of the business world, regarded as a wine industry and business leader.

I wanted to bring my inner and outer lives together, connecting the metaphysical and physical, and integrate my practical need for rationality, for things I could see and prove, with my spiritual desire for approaching the interconnectedness of all things with wisdom and compassion. My public persona and my personal self needed to meld. I had no wish to be one without the other. But business is traditionally about competition, not compassion. Business was dominated by talk of sales metrics and ratios, not Lovingkindness. I worried I would appear ditzy to my business friends.

By chance, while roaming through Portland's Powell's Bookstore, Fritjof Capra's ***The Tao of Physics***, caught my eye. Perched on top of a closeout bin, the metaphysical and science pairing of the title beckoned to me. The back cover proclaimed that the new physics had brought science and spirit together. I bought the book, hoping it held the answer.

Capra, a physicist, set out to show that quantum and sub atomic theory agreed with eastern mysticism, even though the former could be measured and quantified and the latter was intuitive. He argued that the parallels between modern physics and eastern mysticism were compelling enough to infer a merging of science and spirit. Ecology, the science of living systems, claimed that all of nature was interconnected, which Capra pointed out was the essence of spirituality. Capra used the phrase "deep ecology" to express the connection.

Capra's reasoning gave scientific credibility to what naturalists and mystics had been saying for years. Naturalist John Muir wrote in his journal in 1869: "When we try to pick out anything by itself we find that it is bound fast by a thousand invisible cords that cannot be broken, to everything in the Universe." Rudolf Steiner, the founder of biodynamics in the 1920's, tied what happened deep in the earth to the movements of the planets. Both men were considered "far out."

Conventional science remained attached to Isaac Newton's notion of matter as static and Rene Descartes' view of mind and matter as separate entities. Together, Newton and Descartes determined the course of western thought for centuries. Capra and other modern physicists blew apart that tradition by declaring that the universe is composed of units of energy which are not static but in constant motion and part of one great whole.

It struck me as a great cosmic joke that scientists had spent centuries trying to deconstruct the universe and isolate its parts, only to learn that its most significant feature was how interconnected it was. All my paths converged in Capra's book. If scientists could integrate their discipline with metaphysics, the worlds of commerce, business, government, and economics could too. I had to laugh at being so excited about quantum theory when the only high school or college science courses I had taken were the minimum mandated for graduation.

With uncanny timing, two years into my inner journey, I was offered the chance to combine my public and personal selves in an especially visible way. In December, 2009, three years after I had signed away stock control of the winery and almost two years after I had handed over the presidency, I found myself sitting in a corner booth at a local McMinnville restaurant with the Speaker of the Oregon House of Representatives talking about how the local district had become more progressive and less conservative over the past years. He pushed his plate of half-eaten hamburger and French fries to the side and pulled out charts that showed the numbers. I sipped my herb tea, and racked my brain to help him think of who would be a contender in this new environment. After talking for ten minutes, a light bulb went off in my head. He hadn't come to ask my advice. He had come to persuade me to run for the state legislature.

I shouldn't have been surprised. I had once before swerved off the winery path into politics. It was a temporary swerve from which it took years to recover. In 1988, the local Democratic Party had asked me to run for the state legislature. Their arguments sounded reasonable. I had spent two terms on the local school board, had the vineyard under control, and realized that if I wanted to do something about educational policy, it needed to be at the state level. My opponent had never held elected office, although his family was well-known. I wasn't well-known, but the Democratic Party convinced me that my experience as a farmer and owner of a small business, as well as my interest in educational policy, qualified me for the position. I visited the state capitol, with its awe-inspiring chambers, and could imagine myself sitting at one of the desks, making policy for Oregon's future. An open seat gave me a good chance to win. "The election is yours to lose," a prominent Democratic legislator told me.

The campaign of 1988 immersed me in an unfamiliar world. The progressive milieu of the Oregon wine industry had sheltered me from my conservative rural district. I visited homes in all the small communities for campaign "coffees," held to meet voters. The format never varied. Balancing a delicate floral china teacup on my lap, along with my notes of what I wanted to say, I waited for the hostess to introduce me. After I gave my spiel on education, agriculture, and small business, it was time for discussion and questions.

"Do you want a homosexual teaching your kids?" "Do you support killing babies?" The women in flowered print dresses, who had seemed so mild and sweet, went on the attack. Gay rights and abortion were hot button issues. Taken aback and quelling an urge to retort, I said that I thought this election was about bigger issues. That wasn't sufficient. They demanded to know where I stood. "I don't care how good you are. If you are willing to allow homosexual teachers, I can't vote for you," one voter told me. My opponent was active in the state's anti-abortion movement. After a last minute mailer claiming that I supported homosexuality, he won the election. He clearly better represented the voters on the issues they cared about.

I wondered what had made me want to spend that year trying to persuade voters to vote for me, putting myself in the public eye, and opening myself to attacks from all sides. Uncomfortable talking about myself, I put myself in a position where that's all I did. I concluded that in a fit of hubris, I had succumbed to the Democrat's flattery, for which I paid a high price.

I felt ashamed to be defeated by someone who represented everything I was against. Running in a Republican district that had not elected a Democrat in living memory, did not erase my embarrassment. Disappointed and angry at myself for losing an election that should have been mine, I retreated to the confines of my home. How many days, or was it weeks, did I spend, sitting on the living room floor, leaning against the sofa, playing one game of solitaire after another and looking forward to the kids coming home from school to distract me? Finally, I roused myself enough to go outside and start pruning. The vineyard continued its role as my muse and refuge. Outside among the vines, the stillness of the dormant vineyard worked its magic. I started to heal. Two years later I became President of the winery and left politics behind.

In 2009, I was still talked about as a Democratic option, although I'd said no every time the subject of running for office was broached. I listened as the House Speaker told me how electable I was, with the more progressive electorate and my status in the community. My muscles tensed involuntarily and I could feel excitement rise. It would be quite a coup for a Democrat to be elected in this traditionally Republican district. The Speaker had concluded I was the one to make it happen. I knew he was courting me, but maybe he was right. The district really had changed; the incumbent was totally inept; my small business and agriculture experience fit the district perfectly; and Sokol

Blosser was a well known name with a positive reputation. I kept quiet. I couldn't believe I was listening. But I was, as a million thoughts swirled in my head.

I would have to let go of old wounds to enter another political campaign, but maybe this was the opportunity I'd been wanting: an invitation to combine my inner and outer selves in a public way. I sipped my tea as nonchalantly as I could with my head reeling and told the Speaker I'd think about it. Questions kept my mind buzzing. I was concerned about how grueling a campaign would be and whether I was really as electable as he made me sound. I wondered what Russ would say and how this might affect the winery and Alex and Alison. This was a huge decision that would affect not only me but my family and our business and I wasn't even sure how to go about making it.

The invitation to run again came against the backdrop of the Great Recession, which had started in 2008 and sent Oregon reeling. My business experience had repeatedly taught me that crisis meant opportunity if you were willing to face and reframe the issues. Doing this at the state level carried enormous appeal. I could be part of the discussion to reinvent Oregon's economy, bringing my experience in business, agriculture, and sustainability.

These thoughts pulsed through me as I headed home after meeting with the Speaker. Zasu had been waiting in the car and seemed glad to get back in her yard. She raced around and barked at the cars coming down the winery road while I started a walking meditation. I had been told that if you posed a question, then walked in meditation, the answer would rise up inside. I'd never done one, and here was my chance to test it. I asked myself whether I should run for office and started walking slowly back and forth over the bumpy orchard grass. I tried to clear my mind, block out Zasu's barking, and concentrate on slowly placing one foot in front of the other. After about ten minutes, as the weak December sun began to sink behind our giant Sequoia, tears unexpectedly started rolling down my cheeks. A feeling of resignation welled up from deep inside. Talk was cheap. Time to stop complaining and act. If I really cared about the planet and about my community, this was something I could do. As a state legislator, I would have the chance to effect the change I believed necessary. The tears acknowledged what I would have to sacrifice if I chose to run. I wasn't ready to admit it, but the decision was already there, waiting for acceptance.

Wiping my eyes on my coat sleeve, I rubbed Zasu's curly back as we both went back in the house. I didn't tell anyone about my walking meditation, determined to explore rationally the decision my heart had made. I needed to talk to Nik, my politically astute and well-connected son. Nik had been a teenager when I ran in the 1980s and had helped in my campaign. That had turned him on to politics. He went on to be appointed a Page in the United States Congress and had been politically active ever since, masterminding campaigns at the state level. He met another committed "politico," Deborah Kafoury, who became his wife. Before they married, they worked to form X-PAC, a political action committee of young Gen-Xers. Nik went into business for himself, while Deborah became a state legislator. She took time out to have three children and was back in elected office as a county commissioner. Between the two of them, they knew the players and the issues, and were excellent advisors.

Although he had not himself run for office, Nik knew the rigors of a campaign, how difficult my previous campaign had been, and how losing had depressed me. This decision had taken hold of me and I telephoned Nik that same night. My question was this: if I wanted to help move Oregon towards a sustainable economy (sustainable both in terms of environmental responsibility and of continuity) would being a state legislator allow me to do more than my being on advocacy boards like The Nature Conservancy and The Natural Step?

I hoped he would tell me I could do just as much behind the scenes and out of the public eye. Instead he told me to look at the budgets of my boards compared to the state's budget. "Follow the money," he said. "You'd have more power and influence as a legislator." We went back and forth about the whether I should run. I would be running as a Democrat in a conservative Republican district. But the district had changed and my business background gave me bipartisan appeal. A campaign would take time and energy, but I had both. My last campaign had left me miserable, but I was in a different place now.

After about twenty minutes of discussion, Nik finally said, "Mom, I'd like to be able to talk you out of this, but you're the ideal candidate." Not only did he not argue against my running, he fed my hopes. I hung up the phone pondering his advice and wondering what to do next.

"You have your greatest bargaining leverage right now, while you are being wooed," he had said. "Your deciding to do this will make this district much more important, probably a key race. Expect calls from the Governor and other Democratic elected officials persuading you to run. Make sure you extract the financial commitments that you'll need to carry out a successful campaign." The real issues, he told me, were the strength of my opponent, what it would take to run a campaign, and how electable I would be in a traditionally conservative district.

Political campaigns are emotionally battering – as a candidate your life is a fishbowl, and you are subject to potshots at anything you have done in the past. My memoir, ***At Home in the Vineyard***, offered a gift of information to my opponent, but nobody I asked seemed to think there was anything scurrilous in there. "What do I have to be attacked on?" I asked Nik. "It doesn't matter," he said. "If they don't have anything, they'll make it up."

At this point only the incumbent had filed to run. Unless someone in his party filed to run against him, he would be my opponent. The Independent Party of Oregon, after scoring legislators on bipartisan issues, reported that my district's incumbent was the "least effective of all sixty legislators." Local leaders of his party were angry at him for voting against one of their key issues, a transportation package that would have brought significant infrastructure work to the community. The district, which covered the heart of Oregon wine country, had great potential, clearly underserved by its current representative. Everything seemed to point to my running.

My stereotype of a politician was a paunchy hypocrite with a large ego who talked scruples but acted without them. Big money, favors for contributors, basing decisions on getting elected rather than the well-being of the electorate was the popular conception of politicians. Enough elected officials followed the stereotype to keep it going. Running for office in the 1980s, I had been appalled by the amount of self-promotion a campaign involved. Giant egos resulted when politicians started to believe their own propaganda. I didn't want to join that group.

I worried the campaign might turn nasty, remembering the underhanded mailer that helped turn the election in 1988. Machiavellian tactics, winning at all costs, didn't appeal to me. The wine industry in Oregon was known for its collaborative spirit. Competition in my world of business carried a sense of honor. Cutthroat tactics were frowned upon. Those who resorted to them faced retribution in the courts or the marketplace. Even though we were all competitors, we worked together from the beginning to build the reputation of Oregon wine.

In politics, friendly competition doesn't exist, and there is little protection. Negative personal attacks, misrepresenting opponents' positions were commonplace. The difference between competition in business and politics is the difference between Greco-Roman wrestling with its strict rules, and Ultimate Fighting, where anything goes and the victor could end up the most bloodied. If I ran, I wanted to win doing it differently.

I approached Russ with some trepidation, expecting the look of foreboding he gave me when I raised the subject of running for office. "Why would you want to do that? You finally have time to relax. You won't be able to do that if you run for office." His voice grew louder. "I can't believe you're even considering this!" I heard what he had left unsaid. My running for office would take me away from home and from him.

I called my friend Ingrid in San Diego for advice and heard myself wailing. "Russ doesn't want me to do this, but I'm feeling propelled forward. What should I do?" Ingrid was only a few years older but had a wisdom about people that made her my teacher as well as my friend. She surprised me with her perspective on what a political campaign would mean for me. In her mind, my entering a campaign represented a different challenge than just getting elected.

"It's clear you have a gift to give of public service," she told me. "Your challenge is to learn how to offer it so it will be accepted. For one thing," Ingrid told me, in her spiritual yet grounded way, "you have to combine Father Sky and Mother Earth in your campaign to be whole. Just approaching it with your head isn't enough for you. You need to use your heart too."

"Head and heart are not usually combined in politics, Ingrid," I told her. She rebutted. "Combining them is the only way for this to work for you. When you get in the heat of the campaign and the attacks start, you'll want to strike back. That's when you need to learn to respond with Mother Earth rather than Father Sky." I knew what she meant. It was head and heart, the Buddhist dharma of wisdom and compassion. This duality was possible in the business world. I wondered if it would find a place in the ruthless world of politics.

"Next," she went on, "you need to find the balance between your private and public lives. You don't have to choose one at the expense of the other." She was referring to my pattern of going from one extreme to another. Years of intense public activity alternated with periods of reclusiveness. Maybe the pendulum didn't have to swing. If I won it would mean carving out time for myself and my family. If I lost it would mean staying public and not isolating myself.

"Third," Ingrid said, "you've got to include Russ in this decision and in all parts of your life. You are bound together karmically; your mutual healing depends on following this journey together." My reaction at Russ's initial rejection of my idea of running for office had been to think I was in an either-or situation, that I would face a choice. Ingrid said an emphatic "No" to that. That approach was using only head; I needed to include heart. Russ needed to be with me in this decision for me to succeed. We needed to decide together if going through with it would be worth the toll on us.

After laying this groundwork, Ingrid encouraged me to run for office. This suited my expertise, and was an opportunity to grow in important ways. She was very clear that the challenge for me was not winning the election, but was personal growth. If I won without meeting the personal challenges, it would be a hollow victory. "I don't know if you will win," she said. "But for you, this campaign is not about winning. It's about becoming."

I sat down with Russ and told him what Ingrid had said. "I've been thinking too," he said. "Your running for office certainly isn't my first choice, but when you get something in your head, you're a force to reckon with. I'm not going to stop you. I will be here to support you as best I can." I still hadn't made a public commitment, but we had just resolved a key stumbling block.

Zasu was the next hurdle. There was no way I could spend the same amount of time with Zasu and run a campaign. My beautiful dog had come a long way but still needed constant attention. I had a spreadsheet of training activities and marked them off daily. My choice would be extensive day care or giving up Zasu. Lauren, the animal communicator who had become a good friend, helped clear the way. "I don't know why you'd want to run for office," Lauren told me, "but don't worry about Zasu. Her work with you is done. Anyway, your life is going to change. You need to give her up. Call Beth." Lauren's blunt advice liberated me. Releasing Zasu now would not represent failure but rather a fulfillment of her mission. Lauren made me realize it was time for Zasu and me to each take what we had learned and move on.

Beth, who had called Zasu "an awesome dog," while she was training her, agreed to take her as a playmate for her new poodle puppy. Less than a week went by between the decision and the transfer. Before I knew it Russ and I were on our way home from Beth's, our two dog-centered years over. Zasu had been so thrilled at having another poodle to play with, she barely noticed our leaving. It was the right decision for Zasu and for us, yet a soft spot remains in my heart for this puppy, the source of despair at her unruly behavior, but also delight watching her leap through the vineyard. I'd learned an important lesson about choosing a dog. "Don't you ever think about getting another dog," Lauren admonished, "without checking it out with me first."

For months afterward, I would return to my car and expect to see Zasu looking up at me from her perch in the back seat. I called Beth periodically to check on Zasu and found myself relieved to hear that Zasu still barked at cars and raced them along the fence line. "She's the same difficult dog," Beth told me. "But I love her."

15

Campaigning

Ingrid's advice to balance rather than choose between family and career met its first test with Alison. She and I had become closer and more at ease with each other after I ceased being her boss. She consulted me about winery issues and decisions she had to make. I tried to help her think them through. When I forgot and told her what to do, she would remind me to suggest rather than direct. I'd apologize and we'd start over.

When Alison's son, Dario, was born, in May, 2008, I spent as much time as I could with her, first in the hospital, then at home. She had daycare but sometimes brought Dario to stay with me while she went to the winery. His first summer, I often sat with him under our big elm in our wooden glider, holding him in my arms and singing softly as we rocked back and forth. After exhausting my small repertoire of children's songs, I composed new ones, nonsense rhymes to familiar tunes. I'd never been particularly attracted to children, but I found something extraordinary, even magical, about caring for the baby of my baby. My sons both had children whose births I celebrated with delight. But my daughter giving birth was special. I could feel the line of descent, the "through line."

The test came when my decision to run for office dovetailed with the dissolution of Alison's marriage. Early in 2010, when Alison's son was one-and-a-half, her husband left her. The suddenness hit her like a karate chop to the heart. One day, when we were sitting at my kitchen table talking, she blurted out, "I know it's completely selfish, mom," she said, holding back tears, "but I don't want you to run for office. I want you there for me." She couldn't look at me as she said it. "Alison, listen to me," I said, willing her to face me and see I understood. "I am here for you. You can count on me to give you time, emotional support, and physical help."

Alison worked all spring to let go of her attachment to her marriage; I talked to her daily. She'd appear at my back door, stopping on her way to work, her eyes red from crying. "I need a hug, Mom." I'd enfold her in my arms, before sending her on to work, wishing I could impart strength and courage through my embrace, thankful that she felt free to come to me for comfort. It was support I never had.

Bill and I weren't as successful modeling a healthy emotional relationship as we were modeling a work ethic and entrepreneurship. Two of our three children's' first marriages ended in divorce. If children repeat the sins of their parents, perhaps it's progress if they recognize them faster than their parents did. Alison's marriage had uncanny parallels to Bill's and mine. Modeling me, she had repeated my shortcoming. Since she appeared competent and confident in public, I hadn't seen how belittled she'd been at home. She recognized the blessing of her new freedom, that getting out of a controlling relationship was a gift. But she couldn't help being hurt and angry. "Why do I feel so terrible?" she'd ask me. "I know this is the right thing. I don't want to go back. Why can't I let it go?" I had no trouble empathizing. It was the same refrain I'd sung about letting go of the winery.

The spring of 2010, she came down to my house almost every day for lunch, although she didn't have much appetite. Her grief manifested as depression, loss of appetite, and then illness, when she came down with mononucleosis. I watched my daughter shrink from a size eight to a size two. Then, slowly, she started to recover. "I think I'm becoming my own person," she told me, nibbling a peanut butter sandwich. "I feel different. I can't believe how suppressed I was in my marriage." That hit home too. "You're lucky to admit it so soon," I said. "It took me thirty-two years."

She surprised me one day with a new goal. "I want to do a sprint triathlon," she said, answering my quizzical look by explaining it was a partial triathlon. "There's one in Portland this summer and I've signed up." She started training, alternating running, swimming, and cycling, every morning before work. On the day of the event, I went with her and watched as she hit the water for the first leg, streaming along with the pack. When she emerged, dripping and energized, I helped her change into cycling clothes and watched her ride off up the hill. For the final leg, she donned running shoes and took off. I watched anxiously for her return, grinning joyfully when she came into sight and jogged across the finish line, exhausted but victorious.

By mid summer, Alison had rebounded, a tribute to her innate buoyancy. As she found new friends, I saw her less. With fresh confidence, a restored sense of humor, and a reinvigorated outlook, Alison was a new person. Once free of her marriage cocoon, I watched her emerge as a dazzling butterfly.

Alex, friendly yet distant, supported my running, offering suggestions of local people to talk to for support. He was on the board of a local educational nonprofit and gave me the benefit of what he knew about the community. I could feel him still pulling away from me. His twin boys would come over to play Lego, bring their mitts to play catch, or just come talk to me while I was gardening. "Where's your Papa?" I'd ask. "He's at home," or "He's working in the yard," they'd answer. Occasionally I'd test the water and ask Alex if he wanted to have lunch. He was always busy. I missed him, but had to let him go his own way. Nik was spending sixty hours a week building his business and the rest of the time with his three children. He had no leeway to be more than an advisor to my campaign. But he played a critical strategic role from the start, always just a telephone call away.

Running for office took on a life of its own as each concern got resolved. Russ and I went to the state capitol in Salem on filing day for my first public appearance. By that time I was a priority race for the Democratic Party. They had found me a consultant and promised to help hire a campaign manager. If I won, I would be the first Democrat to serve in my district's House seat for over fifty years, except for one two year term in the 1990s. I could hardly believe I was doing this. If someone had told me six months prior that I would be a candidate for the Oregon legislature in the 2010 election, I would have scoffed at such an outlandish prediction.

Once on the campaign trail, I was determined to win. I didn't talk about the personal journey that the campaign represented but, as the campaign got underway, I sat in meditation every morning to center myself, to remind myself of my path, and to ask for guidance. Perched cross-legged on the couch, I wasn't sure who I was asking – God, the universe, personal guides, the life force – but there was something greater than I, and I needed help. To my staff, my consultant, and the Democratic Party, I emphasized this campaign would focus on our district's potential and a vision for moving out of the state's economic crisis. I would hold my opponent accountable but not attack him personally. I would prove it was possible to run a positive campaign.

As I put the pieces of my campaign together, I decided that a political campaign could be the ultimate entrepreneurial experience. It demanded a strategic vision and a business plan, enough early money to begin to execute, then continuing additional investment, all compressed into a short period with a precise, nonnegotiable ending, election day.

Before I had even decided to run, the Democratic Party had introduced me to the campaign consultant from Chicago they wanted me to hire. I didn't think I wanted a consultant from out of state, but I agreed to meet with him over dinner when he came to Portland. He and I were surprised to find we already had a connection – he was a longtime member of the Sokol Blosser Winery Cellar Club. This coincidence seemed to warrant our working together and I got more interested in him. Before deciding, I needed his assurance that it was possible to run the kind of positive campaign I envisioned.

We were sitting at the Dundee Bistro, the local winery hangout, had ordered our dinners, and it was time for my big question. "I want to run an honorable campaign," I said. "One I can hold my head up high after winning. I don't want to engage in scurrilous attacks, but I see so much of that. Is it possible to win with a positive campaign?"

"Absolutely," he said immediately. "You can hold the incumbent accountable for his record," he said, "and still run a positive campaign." That cinched my decision on the spot. The wine came and we toasted to the success of our collaboration with, what else, but Sokol Blosser Pinot Noir.

Hiring a campaign manager proved more difficult. After offering the job and being turned down by two different people, I was feeling desperate. Then Ryan appeared. Young and earnest, Ryan had never run a legislative campaign before. He had just graduated from Oregon State University where he had been student body president, so I knew he had politics in his blood. He was thrilled to get the job. "I won't let you down," he said when I hired him. And he didn't. I was almost old enough to be his grandmother but he ran my life during the campaign.

Campaigns run on dollars. I thought I knew about fundraising from my previous campaign, but it didn't take me long to realize that campaigns had changed and I had no idea what I was getting into. Raising money would be front and center. Nik had a friend who was an experienced fundraiser, had worked with the current governor and other political figures, and was willing to help me. Jef became a key figure in my campaign. He set up a fundraising structure, taught me how to "make the ask," found names of potential donors who might resonate with my message, sat with me during the hours of calling, made appointments for me to meet with Portland business leaders, accompanied me on fundraising visits, and kept the fundraising records. He and Ryan, one a University of Oregon alum, the other from Oregon State, kept their intercollegiate competition alive with lighthearted banter that filled the campaign office with laughter.

The first days of calling were excruciating. I lay awake at night with my teeth clenched. I disliked asking friends and family for money, and months of fundraising lay ahead. I suggested recruiting others to ask on my behalf, but both Nik and Jef squashed that idea. "People want to be asked by the candidate," they told me. "No one is going to be able to do this but you." After accepting that reality, I swallowed hard and kept at it. I stopped being embarrassed and learned to be straightforward about why I was running and what I thought I would bring to the legislature. I wanted people to feel that by donating to my campaign, they were investing in a better future for Oregon. Jef connected me with people who followed politics and understood campaigns. Often, after thanking them for their support, they surprised me by thanking me back. "I agree with what you stand for," one businessman told me. "But I couldn't do it. Thank you for putting yourself out there."

I started using this when I spoke to business groups, giving them five reasons why they should support me. My number one reason: "I'm running so you don't have to." Business friends in Portland were enthusiastic about seeing my business experience added to the state legislative makeup. Money flowed in. During that summer, the political reporter for ***The Oregonian*** commented that my contribution list looked like a ***Who's Who*** of the Portland business community. Supporters liked to position me as "giving back to the community" by running for office, but I didn't feel altruistic. We were facing an economic/social/environmental crisis and I wanted to be part of creating policy to get us out of it.

There was not as much money locally, but that's where the votes were. I visited the small businesses up and down the main street of McMinnville to introduce myself and listen to the challenges they faced. I went to talk to local business leaders, mostly Republicans, to explain why I was running and why I was a good fit to represent the district. I asked for their support and a financial investment in my campaign. My high success rate kept me energized.

Among farmers, I discovered a disparity in interests and needs between the older conventional farmers and the younger organic ones. The former sold their crops on the global commodity market, growing them locally and shipping them through commodity brokers. The organic farmers, chiefly younger and new to farming, sold their produce locally. This new local food supply fueled farmers markets and local restaurants. The trend of young people deciding to go into market-direct farming represented a key piece of a new economy and the revitalization of agriculture. They reminded me of my cohort of young urban professionals who started the wine industry in the 1970s.

Innumerable union meetings taught me the issues of the building trades, the state police, teachers, and public employees. An incumbent had the advantage of already knowing the issues. I had to hustle to understand the concerns of each group, decide what to emphasize, and think through how to deal with each, knowing that I probably would not support one hundred per cent of any faction. As a Democrat, broad union support came easily, although I made clear when I went to union meetings that I was also a business owner. Business and labor needed to work together.

Talking to voters individually mitigated the unpleasantness of candidate forums. The more I could avoid my opponent, the happier I was. When I wasn't fundraising or meeting community leaders, I was out walking the district and knocking on doors. Canvassing was a centerpiece of Democratic Party campaigns; talking with voters, meeting them at their homes, and asking for their vote, showed them how important they were. I was expected to canvass on a regular basis until the end. Uncomfortable making small talk, I wasn't looking forward to knocking on strangers' doors. Jef told me that after spending the day calling people asking for money, I would start looking forward to my late afternoon, early evening walk talking to voters. He was right.

Most people who decided to answer their door were not particularly interested in me or the election. But there were exceptions. In the months of walking the district, I met voters who were thrilled that I had taken the time to come talk to them personally, and voters who said they would never vote for me since I was a Democrat. I chanced upon the woman who had taken care of Nik, almost forty years earlier, when he was a toddler in daycare at the First Presbyterian Church. "I've been following your career," she said, "and I'm thrilled you're running. I'm behind you 100 percent." That was a good day.

I knocked on the door of retired teachers who had had Nik or Alex or Alison in grade school or high school. I met the woman who had cut my mother's hair during her last years and others who had played golf, bridge, or Mahjong with her and remembered her fondly. I was reaping a harvest of good feelings various members of my family had engendered over nearly half a century in the community.

Canvassing also served as a reality check. Since I spent most of my time with supporters, getting out to visit voters in different neighborhoods gave me a better overall view of the mood of the electorate. The recession was in full bloom and the mood ranged from depressed to surly. Many were home because they had been laid off. People blamed the President, Congress, and the state legislature for taxing them too much, especially the Democrats, who they saw as the root of the problem. In the next breath, they complained that the government didn't do enough.

Canvassing got me home too late to enjoy our garden. The peas, spinach, and carrots I had planted before the campaign got underway became crowded by weeds and went to seed. I found myself working more than full-time for a job that was only part-time and paid little. "What's wrong with this picture?" I asked myself. There was no satisfactory answer. I had to keep going. If I lost, I didn't want to look back and wonder if I'd just made a few more phone calls or canvassed a few more houses....

Any hope of getting by without being attacked turned out to have been fantasy. I had thought that with my business background, I could break through party ranks. Instead I ran up against a determined state Republican lobby who vowed to do whatever it took to keep a legislative seat they considered theirs. I was glad to have someone to turn to, to help me weather the shadow side of campaigning. Every time I was slammed or the winery was attacked, I notified my campaign consultant. No matter whether it was morning, night, holiday, weekend, he called me back immediately. His calm voice told me to "Stay on message. Ignore their tactics. They're trying to distract you. Don't let yourself get dragged into their game and get control of the campaign. Right now they're reacting to you. Stay in control."

The attacks started early and continued nonstop. I didn't expect them until the last weeks of the campaign and should have been flattered to have been considered a threat so early. It became obvious that the goal of my opponent's campaign was to destroy me so that, by comparison, their candidate would look good. They started with attacks on Sokol Blosser Winery. The campaign had barely gotten underway when, during the winery's Memorial Weekend Open House, some of our visitors asked who the people were carrying signs at the entrance to the winery road. We went down to look. There, at the entrance to the winery driveway, were a group of picketers, with signs that said: *This winery favors higher taxes*, and *Susan Sokol Blosser is pro abortion*. Both statements sounded ridiculous, but the half dozen picketers carried their signs with self-righteous fervor.

Furious that my political campaign was intruding on winery business, especially on one of our big weekends, I ran to the phone to call my consultant.

"It's one thing to attack me and another to attack the business! This is so unethical. Should I call anyone, maybe the newspaper or the sheriff?" The picketers played into my fears that running for office would negatively affect the winery.

"Don't call anyone," he told me. "They would love newspaper coverage. Don't let them have it. Just make sure they aren't endangering cars or customers and let them be." This calmed me down. Alex reassured me that the picketers were not our customers anyway, and they hadn't stopped the flow of visitors to the winery. I was still upset. In my mind attacking my business was out of line.

Another week picketers appeared again with signs: *Sokol Blosser Winery hires illegal aliens.* Prejudice against our Mexican community hit a new low in the campaign as immigration surfaced as a rallying cry for my opponent. A statement I made in my book, ***At Home in the Vineyard,*** in which I lamented the labor situation I faced in the 1980s, was twisted to make it appear that the winery's practice was to intentionally hire illegal immigrants. Despite explanations at forums, in mailers to voters, and in the newspaper, my opponent deliberately distorted what I had written and this issue gained momentum.

This was a "Have you stopped beating your wife?" type of accusation. If you don't beat your wife, how do you answer? You're immediately on the defensive, forced to explain that you don't beat your wife and can't even imagine it. I was repeatedly put in this position, with allegations that I was pro-abortion, would raise taxes, would knuckle under to the Democratic leadership on votes, hired illegal workers, and was part of the liberal Portland community.

Early in the summer, Alex caught a film crew trespassing in our vineyard, starting to film an ad for my opponent. A blond-haired woman, whom we later found out was a paid actress, was standing in our vineyard waving my book and telling the camera that, "Susan Sokol Blosser hired illegal immigrants."

When Alex confronted them, they pleaded ignorance. "Isn't this public property?"

"No, it isn't," Alex replied. "Vineyards are not public property and you're in the middle of ours." He asked them to leave and called the Sheriff to report it. Incensed at another attack on my business, adrenalin flowed with the urge to retaliate. Ingrid's advice not to lash out and strike back echoed in my mind.

Throughout the summer, my opponent's staff had a camera aimed at me. Whether I was looking or not, they snapped pictures. They must have accumulated quite a portfolio. When I complained to my staff, Ryan explained, "They're after the most unflattering picture they can get to use against you later." We knew they'd found it when a mailer attacking me appeared with such an unattractive photo I hated to admit it was me. I realized how important my race had become when a capitol lobbyist revealed that powerful state Republicans had told my opponent to keep his head down and do what they told him to do; they would take over the campaign.

We laughed at some of the allegations they came up with to make me sound unappealing, especially the one accusing me of being "against global warming."

"They finally hit on one that's true," I exclaimed. Nik told me my opponent's strategists would throw everything they could think of at me to see what would stick. They settled on immigration as the issue with the most resonance among district voters, a sad commentary of discrimination against a group of people critical to our community.

We asked respected members of each area of the district to write letters of support to mail to their neighbors. I made sure these letters contained only reasons to support me, with no mention of my opponent. The opposition sent out letters too, notable for slamming me. People who had never met me wrote letters lambasting me for things they could have had no knowledge of, primarily because they were untrue. The letters were probably written by party strategists, but that doesn't excuse the individuals who signed them. One came from a pastor of a fundamentalist church, reminding me that Christian did not necessarily equal honorable.

As the attacks rolled in, I tried to practice Buddhist equanimity, but the constant pummeling took its toll. It depressed me to see such unsavory tactics aimed squarely at me. My opponent portrayed me as a criminal so many times, I feared people would assume it was true. Even Nik, inured to the vicissitudes of campaigning, was upset by the trumped up accusations. He thought he discovered an Oregon statute which might protect me from such libel and urged me to bring suit, which I did in the last weeks of the campaign. TV news and right wing talk shows swooped down after I filed suit. My opponent played the victim, protesting he was innocent of any wrongdoing and my suit was another political ploy. Irate that he was trying to position himself as the injured party, I was ready to forge ahead when, much to my dismay, I learned the election laws didn't protect me after all. I had to drop the suit, which my opponent jumped on as proof of his position. My morning meditation became increasingly important. I kept reminding myself that my challenge in this campaign was to fight with my heart as well as my head, to conquer through compassion rather than anger. I could not let myself stoop to my opponent's level.

Emotional yoyo would be a good description of my months of campaigning. In the space of one day, I'd experience depression seeing an attack flier, or being yelled at by an angry voter; and then elation at receiving an unexpected contribution and note of support, getting a newspaper endorsement, surviving a joint appearance. The positive happenings kept me buoyed and optimistic. An event that later took on a life of its own was a dinner fundraiser I did in September, the height of harvest season. The revitalization of agriculture was one of my campaign themes, so when a farmer friend called to say she'd donate some of her famous heirloom chickens if I wanted to have a fundraiser, I got the idea of featuring not only her chicken but the whole cornucopia of products from our district. We called it Bounty of the County. We got all the food and wine locally, and featured some of the young farmers whose stories were compelling. I had no trouble selling all the tables. People loved the idea of a "good news" event highlighting a positive trend in agriculture. They also knew any event at Sokol Blosser would have great wine and food. Indeed, we set a new culinary benchmark for a political fundraiser. Conventional campaign fare – greasy corn dogs, gloppy potato salad, and sugary sheet cake – had no place in my campaign.

Served family style, Bounty of the County was a seasonal feast. Platters of heirloom tomatoes and fresh mozzarella, salads of organic greens, fresh corn on the cob, succulent little lamb chops, and fresh peach tarts with organic whipped cream covered every space of the tables that weren't covered by glasses of Oregon Pinot Noir. When I sought items for a silent auction, I was overwhelmed with the generosity of the local wineries who donated their best. Bounty of the County became a highlight of my campaign. It was a win-win, raising significant funds while articulating my vision for the district. The setting, the quality of the food, and the energy of the event generated considerable buzz in political circles.

The week before the election I sat in a secluded corner of my campaign office, a sheaf of names in my lap, personally calling voters who had been identified through previous canvassing as undecided. A personal call from me was a last ditch effort to win them over. My telephone headset felt like an extra appendage. Going door to door was still a campaign priority, but not for me. We had a group of canvassers spread out over the entire district, both on foot and on the phone, in a giant get-out-the-vote effort, masterminded by Nik, who took time off to come help me in the last days. Alex and Alison also pitched in with last minute calls to voters. As we neared the end of the campaign, the polls showed we were pulling ahead. This time I was going to win.

I arranged to share an election night party with a spirited Yamhill County Commissioner who was about to save her seat in a hard fought battle with a "tea party" opponent. We rented McMinnville's Grand Ballroom. Nik and Deborah came, having arranged to spend the night in McMinnville. Supporters filed in early to celebrate, causing the four cases of wine I had brought to disappear within an hour. Conversation was lively as guests enjoyed hors d'oeuvres and sweets contributed by local chefs. I couldn't stop glancing at the big clock on the wall, knowing the first numbers would be posted soon. Nik was monitoring them.

Shortly after 8:00, Nik beckoned to me to come down the hall to the Democratic Party office. Following him, eager to hear the first results, I stopped short on entering the room. My staff and our loyal canvassers, seated in the midst of old pizza boxes and empty soda cans, looked up at me with tears in their eyes. Nik told me what the staff already knew.

"Mom," he said. "The first returns are in. Enough to decide the election." He looked at me sorrowfully. "You lost." He put his arm around me. "I'm so sorry." Dazed and shattered, I stood, silently taking in Nik's words. How could that be? This was to be my victory party. I couldn't have lost again. The past months of total devotion to the campaign – all the fundraising, knocking on doors, phoning voters, unpleasant candidate forums, vicious attacks – had been for nothing.

A bipartisan mix of community leaders seldom seen together at a political gathering stood in the next room. I felt so lucky to have all these good people behind me. Yet I had lost, even with such great support. It would take all my backbone to tell them the news. As I made my way to the microphone, Judge Collins told me a quick story. After Adlai Stevenson lost the presidential election to Dwight Eisenhower in 1952, someone tried to comfort him by saying that at least he had all the thinking people behind him. Stevenson responded "Yes, but I needed a majority." That summed up how I felt.

As I took the microphone, a calm numbness flowed through me, cloaking my chagrin, as I shared the news. I looked out at the crowd of friendly faces and watched as a mantle of gloom erased their happy chatter. I thanked my staff and supporters with all the grace I could muster. Then my family whisked me away to the back room at Nick's Italian Cafe.

I sent an email to all my contributors and volunteers thanking them for their support. A flood of letters responded. A local McMinnville pastor wrote: "Susan, your ethical campaign has raised the level of dialogue and participation within this county....As a citizen and a new friend, I want to thank you for your leadership in our county."

An attorney acquaintance wrote: "I am writing to say that you are to be congratulated on an excellent campaign. It is difficult to understand how you lost considering your obvious superiority over your opponent."

Another wrote: "It takes a lot of guts to run for office where your integrity and core values are challenged, where your life beliefs are in full view and become subject to attack. I admire you for the energy, emotion and skill you put into your bid for office...." I kept a stack of these cards in a special cubbyhole in my desk.

I didn't understand what had happened to my winning trajectory. I did realize that a Republican tsunami had flooded the country in the last two weeks of the 2010 election. Democrats of all stripes, liberal and conservative, were either swept out of office or denied entry; not one of my Democratic challenger colleagues, all of whom were projected to win, crossed the finish line victorious. A former state legislator who had helped me canvass summed it up: "You waged a really good campaign. There were larger forces in motion that demolished even the best efforts."

Knowing we were part of a larger national context didn't absolve the savagery of my campaign. Russ, who had seen me devote everything to the campaign for the last ten months, was irate at my opponent's underhanded tactics. He wrote a letter to the editor, excoriating the deception, fabrications, and mudslinging. He held off mailing it, deciding he'd better show it to Alex and Alison because of his connection to the winery. They persuaded him to sit on it. I agreed, although I admired the letter. His concern for me, his passion for fairness, and the biting wit with which he wrote, was quintessential Russ.

When I lost my bid for election in 1988, I was totally deflated. A campaign was a competition. The best person should come out on top. When it wasn't me, I took the loss personally. In 2010, although the sting of losing was no less intense, defining the campaign as a journey changed my perspective.

I had run the campaign I wanted. In that respect, I was successful. All three newspapers which considered my race, endorsed me, including ***The Oregonian***, which went beyond its regular jurisdiction to do so. I had the support of prominent community leaders, Republican and Democrat. People stopped me in the street: "I can't believe you lost! You're such a good fit for the district. How did this happen?"

When Russ had first compared my credentials with those of my opponent at the start of the campaign, he commented I was so much better qualified that there should be no contest. "That's why you play the game," he added. How right he was. Losing hurt. My ego suffered the agony of defeat. But underneath the hurt, my commitment to the community had grown. I wasn't sorry I had run. The concerned, caring people I met made me appreciate my community more than ever.

I thought about Ingrid's advice given many months before about integrating my public and private lives. My campaign had built up considerable momentum and community spirit. Rather than retreat and isolate myself as I had done in the past, I needed to act, to seize the opportunity and build on the energy of my campaign. Maybe I could work locally on what I was denied the chance to do at the state level. Ingrid and I hadn't spoken since I'd decided to run. I wanted to see her, to ask her advice. She invited me to visit her right away in San Diego and I went.

I recounted the enthusiastic energy of my staff and supporters; the incredible bipartisan support I had; the impressive amount of money I raised; and how I had reconnected to a community I loved and had been away from while focused on winery business. "I ran a textbook campaign. I should have won. I can't believe I lost," I told her. "You didn't lose," she said. "Your campaign was a dress rehearsal."

"Huh? What do you mean, 'dress rehearsal'?'"

"You needed the campaign to lay the groundwork for what comes next," she said. "Whatever that is."

16

Bhutan

Back home, the sting of my loss lingered. I wanted to get over it, to move on. On a whim, I emailed Kim Stafford, an Oregon writer from whom I'd taken several writing workshops. "I need to exorcise my campaign; I think writing will help," I wrote. "What classes are you teaching next?" With characteristic kindness, he responded right away. "I've attached my teaching schedule, but the best thing for you is to get away. I'm leading a writer's trip to Bhutan. Why don't you come with me and bring your husband?" I reread his invitation to make sure I had read it right. A beautiful invitation had just landed in my lap. Maybe this was just what I needed. For the first time in weeks, a big smile spread across my face.

I had to consult a world map to find out where Bhutan, a country I'd barely heard of, was located. The more I learned, the more enthusiastic I became. This was a tiny Buddhist country, the Switzerland of the Himalayas, whose beloved King, in an unprecedented royal act, had abdicated the throne in favor of his son. I wondered if he had had trouble letting go. He measured the well-being of his people by Gross National Happiness (GNH) rather than Gross National Product (GNP) and struggled to maintain their culture by strictly limiting foreign visitors. This was a land where Buddhism seeped into every nook and cranny. What an adventure it would be to visit. I couldn't wait to tell Russ, who, characteristically, pointed out the drawbacks. I had an answer for each one.

He: "I'm not sure I can go; I'll be preparing for a bottling then."
Me: "Your cellar crew can take care of it. You've trained them well."

He: "I'm not a writer. What will I do when you're writing?"

Me: "The other spouses aren't writers either. There will be plenty to do."

He: "Who will take care of the cats?"
Me: "I'll ask Lily and Rick to stay. The cats like them."

He: "You have to fly to Tokyo, then Bangkok. You'll be on planes for twenty-four hours! And look how expensive it is."
Me: "This is a chance of a lifetime."

Four days later, "Will you still go if I don't?"
"Yes, I think I would."
He paused. "God dammit, Mabel. You can't go alone. I'm going with you."
"Thank you, George," I said primly.

We scrambled to renew our passports, both of which had just expired, get shots, read recommended books, and buy trekking poles. We left in late January, glad to put Russ's winery concerns and my campaign malaise behind.

Forty hours after leaving Portland, our small Drukair plane dove down into the narrow Paro Valley, the one spot flat enough for a jet to land. Our magical journey had begun.

A mantle of Buddhism floats over Bhutan. The giant golden statue of the Buddha on a hillside near Thimpu sends a message and a welcome to Bhutan, like the Statue of Liberty does for the United States, each symbolizing the character of the nation. Omnipresent prayer flags, lashed to homes, strung along roadways, even on mountain tops, sustained the feeling. Prayer wheels twirled throughout the country, in town centers and on country pathways. Their messages of peace and goodwill, blew in every direction. People we met lived these values. Despite clear beautiful rivers, fly fishing was not popular. "We've had requests for fly fishing trips, but we don't like to do them," our guide told us. "Why would you want to hurt the fish?" On one occasion, we saw him take a bug he found inside, and gently let it go outside. "That's something I would do," Russ said approvingly.

We were twelve international travelers in Kim's group, bobbing across Bhutan in a small bus. The weather was cold and clear. We shared the single paved lane of Bhutan's transnational highway with a procession of motorized vehicles of all shapes and sizes, from tiny tractors to highly decorated dump trucks. Cows, dogs, and pedestrians joined the traffic stream as well, each on a journey of its own. Spiraling up and down the mountainous terrain, each corkscrew curve on the one lane road offered another peril. We marveled at the composure of our Bhutanese driver who held our lives in his hands.

At medieval fortresses, we climbed gingerly up impossibly steep, wooden steps, concave with the passage of so many feet. Extravagant, intricately colored murals and geometric designs covered every available space in venerable structures where church and state lived together. Red-robed monks chanted in one section while government staff did business in another.

Billed as a writers' journey, the highlight of our trip was reaching Ogyen Choling, family home of Bhutan's first woman novelist, Kunzang Choden, who joined us for the weekend. Part of the experience was getting there. We drove far into the countryside, then left our bus and hiked uphill on a dirt path in the cold clear air for two hours to reach the 14th century feudal castle. Small cottages with terraced farming, growing buckwheat in tiny triangular plots, dotted the hillside. When we reached the compound and were assigned rooms, Russ and I found ourselves in the "Altar Room," a wood-walled room with two narrow beds, two small windows, a few hooks for coats, and a tiny bukhari wood stove. A wooden altar, with its faded, timeworn ornamentation, was the only remnant of the original religious room of the ancient building. We slept in our long underwear, grateful for the hot water bottles that appeared on our beds every night.

For the next two days, our group sat in the gathering room, close to the smoky bukhari stove, writing on our own or using Kim's "prompts." A prompt that hit home was to write about the importance of failure. Behind honors and accomplishments, Kim explained, lay an understory. "What the world sees as success," he told us, "is the final manifestation of struggle, faltering, failure." I understood. The outward success of Sokol Blosser Winery's generational transition masked my struggle underneath. There was an understory of pain and anguish behind what was publicly honored for being smooth and seamless. It seemed to me the reverse could also be true, that the understory of failure could reveal honor. My election defeat had an understory of running an honorable campaign.

Our trip to Bhutan was indeed the trip of a lifetime. What started as an adventure turned into an inner journey for both Russ and me. Russ came home with what he called his "Bhutan calm." I returned feeling healed, ready to put politics behind me, permanently.

17

Next

I couldn't decide if running for office in 2010 proved I was an eternal optimist or just a slow learner. Whichever it was, I was ready to finally accept that elected politics was not my venue for public service. While the idea of having to go before the voters made sense, having to seek votes put me in the "pleaser" position, my nemesis. I realized I could work to better my community without compromising my personal self.

I wanted to stay engaged, to find a way to channel the momentum generated by my campaign and work on the issues I cared about. If it weren't as an elected official, I needed to fine another route. I looked at starting a small business and then decided that a nonprofit with tax-exempt status, that could apply for grants and accept donations, would be the best solution. Encouraged by friends, I started planning my next venture.

Yamhill County, where I lived, had so much going for it. As the heart of the Oregon wine industry, it had become a wine tourism destination which, in turn, attracted top chefs and other tourism amenities. These in turn attracted manufacturers, builders, designers, and other suppliers. Yet, the poverty level was high, the local food bank needed donations, and several local churches offered weekly community dinners to help feed people. There was no end of potential projects I could tackle. I decided to build a name for my enterprise around the acronym YES, which stood for the Yamhill Enrichment Society, benign and broad enough to serve as an umbrella for diverse projects.

Incorporating YES as a public benefit company in the state of Oregon, and donating my leftover campaign funds to YES, I put politics behind me. When Oregon's Speaker of the House (the person who first approached me to run) called to ask me to give my surplus campaign money to the Democratic Party, I was able to tell him, with only a twinge of guilt, that my remaining funds were already in my nonprofit's bank account.

As I went around to talk to people with whom I wanted to work, I realized how much my campaign had laid the foundation for this new project. Ingrid was right. I wouldn't have had this idea pre-campaign. I also would not have had the same support. My campaign had raised my visibility and stature. Each of the community leaders I spoke with lit up with visible interest as we talked. Busy people were willing to make room in their schedules and join this new enterprise.

The projects I envisioned for YES ranged wide, encompassing music enrichment, agriculture, early childhood literacy, women's issues, community history. I articulated YES's mission as "to enrich our community by supporting projects in education and the arts, food and agriculture, history, and community" with the tag line "building community through innovation and collaboration." YES provided the opportunity to combine cultural projects, economic development, and environmental concerns, three key interests, within a framework of compassion and activism. Both my public and personal selves could flower under YES's umbrella.

When I was president of Sokol Blosser Winery, I considered it the zenith of my life. I couldn't imagine not doing it. Now I saw it was just part of my journey, giving me the credibility to move to a new stage. If I had focused during the transition on what I would do, I would not have arrived at YES.

By this time, it had been almost three years since I had left Sokol Blosser Winery. My office sat unused, my things taking up space and gathering dust. My phone line, which for years had blinked with multiple messages, sat silent and dark. Alex and Alison weren't pushing, but it was time for them to make use of space reserved for me at the winery and for me to move my base of operations to McMinnville.

Mission control for my campaign had been the first floor of an old Victorian house in downtown McMinnville. Converted to offices, it was ideally placed for me, two blocks from the small shops and restaurants lining McMinnville's historic main street. I could walk to meet someone for coffee or lunch, pick up last minute groceries, do banking, fill a prescription, even buy clothes. I loved living on the vineyard, but being part of a walkable urban community gave me the best of both worlds.

The office break became final when I rented the large front room upstairs in the Victorian house. My handyman husband painted the walls, installed shelving in the closet, moved furniture, and got me comfortably settled. We made use of what remained of my mother's living room furniture. The two old Queen Anne wing-back chairs from my childhood fit the ambiance of the old house. Mother's large carved wooden Chinese wall hanging took a place of honor on my office wall. What would have looked out of place in Russ's and my home, looked welcoming in my office. I loved having my own space, a "room of my own", to work out of. At the winery, my former office was dismantled, installed with a conference table and christened "The Founders' Room." After a few years, Alison took it over as her office.

Three months after the election, my YES board members crowded around the conference table in the new office, discussing what "building our community through innovation and collaboration" could look like. The energy in the air was palpable. I proposed a number of projects that interested me. Some captured their attention, others not so much. The ones I could persuade them to get behind, we took on. One board member, with young children of her own, told us about a childhood literacy project she'd dreamed about starting. She persuaded us to take that on too.

Our enthusiasm coalesced around six diverse projects to pursue our first year. Books for Babies would provide every new baby born at the Willamette Valley Medical Center with a new book for parents to read to it, including a message on why it was so important to read to babies. Koncert for Kids would bring music enrichment first to McMinnville elementary students and later to the rural areas of the county. Women's leadership luncheons would bring Yamhill County women of different generations and professions together to share stories. Living History would focus on daily life in McMinnville 100 years ago, with old photographs and a tour of historic homes. Agriculture would take two tacks: first a food collaborative to help build a robust local food economy; second a celebration of Yamhill County's unique trifecta of talented chefs, small, diversified family farms, and famous wines. We were going to make Yamhill County a culinary destination. My Bounty of the County campaign fundraiser would take on a new life as a Yamhill County culinary showcase and fundraiser for YES.

I conducted YES business from my laptop computer sitting at my mother's tall secretary desk, listening to classical music, loving my freedom and my own space. When Russ left in the morning to walk up the hill to work at the winery, I got in the car and drove to my McMinnville office. By the end of our first year, we had accomplished our initial goals and were able to expand each of the six programs.

YES started me on a new path of entrepreneurship. I had finally accepted that term. While Bill and I were building our business, I regarded the word entrepreneur as an insult. To me, entrepreneurs were the robber barons of the late 19th century, risk takers seeking profit without regard to people or planet. They represented the antithesis of my triple bottom line (people, planet, profit). Then, in 2008, members of the Oregon Entrepreneurs Network nominated me for Entrepreneur of the Year. When I went to be interviewed, I questioned whether I should be there, protesting that I wasn't really an entrepreneur since money was not my motivation. I gave them copies of ***At Home in the Vineyard*** so they could see how far I was from the conventional definition. They responded by making me one of their three finalists for the year.

Russ donned his tux and I my mother's rhinestone earrings for their glamorous awards dinner. We sat in a hotel ballroom with the other 998 guests and saw me larger than life on a giant screen when they showed video interviews of each finalist before announcing the winner.

Despite feeling I didn't belong there, I found myself disappointed the winning name was not mine. The experience, however, did revise my views. Maybe an entrepreneur could be about more than money. Innovation and risk were also key components of entrepreneurship. Under that definition, I was one. Without a challenge to believe in, I am at loose ends, bored, restless. With one, I have enormous energy and focus.

After I lost the election, my brother Henry had called with condolences. At the end of our conversation he said: "You'll find another mountain to climb." Founding the Yamhill Enrichment Society turned out to be my new climb, ushering in the entrepreneurship of the elder. What put YES in this new category was that this climb was not about ascending the ladder of career success, not about accumulation. Rather, it was about giving away, using what I had gained to add to the quality of life in my community, what I have come to see as the role of the elder. This time I vowed not to let it take over my life. I would expand my garden, play with my grandchildren, sit and read more, take up needlepoint again, and enjoy my small flock of hens who race over when I appear, wanting to be first in case I'd brought corn. Maybe, with Lauren's help, I'd even get another puppy.

When I turned over the presidency in 2008, I left Bill's and my presidential papers in file cabinets. Together, our papers traced the ups and downs of the business, with harvest and production records, sales and marketing plans, financial projections and actuals, legal issues, vineyard records. Everything that the winery did for the thirty-seven years that Bill and I ran the business resided in those papers. I realized how far removed from the winery I had become when I went back to find something from my files and they weren't where I had left them. When I inquired, I found that except for current contracts, all the old papers had been removed. Alex and Alison had found themselves short of space, and decided to clean house. They had put old records in storage but really wanted to throw out as much as they could.

I couldn't let them do that; the history of the early wine industry in Oregon would be lost to future generations. It was already looking different than it had only ten years earlier. As founders of the Oregon wine industry, our records might someday help historians reconstruct its origins.

I knew how valuable primary sources could be. As an old history major and former archivist, the past remained both relevant and important. I wanted the papers of the early vintners to be preserved. McMinnville's Linfield College, with its new Center for the Northwest, its historic hosting of the annual International Pinot Noir Celebration, and its wine aficionado president, would be the perfect place to house the history of the Oregon wine industry. When I proposed the opportunity to start a repository of Oregon wine history to Linfield's president, his face lit up with interest. He wasted no time finding a donor, outfitting a climate controlled space, hiring an archivist, and establishing the Oregon Wine History Archives.

Linfield's wine industry archival project began in 2011 with the donation of records from Sokol Blosser's first thirty-five years. I personally packed up boxes of early correspondence, old vineyard records, marketing plans, photographs, and financial particulars, which got carted off to be archived for posterity, on temperature controlled shelves, in twenty-eight linear feet of boxes. Linfield's original goal was to get the papers of six of the early couples: the Ponzis, Letts, Adelsheims, Redfords, Eraths, and Sokol Blossers. Records from our era would be the last ones on actual paper. The future was electronic. Encouraged by the response to their project, Linfield procured grants to expand their scope. They got the archives of the early editions of the ***Oregon Wine Press***, and engaged students to procure oral histories from some of the Latino workers who were critical to building the industry.

Helping preserve the early history of the Oregon wine industry circled me back forty years to the beginnings of my career as a historian. This time I participated in both ends of the historical continuum: I both made history and preserved it.

Removing my presidential papers from Sokol Blosser was one more step in erasing my presence at the winery. Although the staff welcomed me when I appeared, so much had changed; so many new faces. As the Founder, I was invited to meet with new hires to tell them how the winery started and its early days. I represented the past. The present and future of the winery belonged to Nik, Alex, and Alison. I wouldn't have had it otherwise. Yet it felt bittersweet. I didn't want to go back, but couldn't help thinking fondly of the days when I had been the winery's Grand Poobah.

18

Mother-Daughter

Five and a half years after giving up the presidency of Sokol Blosser, I pulled into a parking space at a hotel in Oregon wine country just as Alison pulled up next to me. She was a married woman again, having remarried the year before. I watched her check her iPhone, give a big sigh, grab her purse, and ease her pregnant belly out of her car.

"How are you feeling?" I asked as we started walking towards the hotel. Together, as a mother-daughter team, we were the keynote speakers at the national conference of Women for WineSense.

"Okay, just tired," the seven months pregnant co-president of Sokol Blosser Winery said. "It's been a long day."

I sympathized. The unending demands of running a business were tiring under any circumstances. How glad I was to no longer deal with those demands. As we made our way along the rose bordered pathway, companionably chatting, I thought how much I treasured the rapport I had with my daughter. We had an ease of sharing I wished for but never had with my own mother.

The first years after Mother died, I seldom thought about her, relieved that her judging voice inside me had receded. Then she'd surface at odd moments. I'd find that voice coming out of my own mouth, telling Alison what to do. She closed down just as I had, then learned to tease me until I realized what I was doing and we could both laugh.

I was surprised to find myself suddenly thinking about and missing my mother, lamenting that we had not been able to get past our control issues to meet on equal footing. Thwarting her attempts to dominate me had cut her out of much of my life. Deliberately keeping our conversations superficial wasn't hard. There was still plenty to talk about as we shared a number of interests. I sought her advice on knitting patterns; we chatted about her cat; looked up the various birds that came to her feeders; discussed dieting. Family stories were a dependable fallback. An ongoing conversation was trying to decide when Daddy's Alzheimer's first started. I grew adept at changing the subject if she asked me again why I left Bill, or anything else I didn't want to share with her. She told me I was being secretive because I was a Scorpio.

Being a Scorpio had nothing to do with my denying my mother what she wanted to know about me. I chose not to tell her personal things for fear of reprisal. Yet I yearned for that closeness, making Alison's confiding in me all the sweeter. Years after Mother died, I started to wish I knew more about what mattered to her. Subjects we had never discussed kept occurring to me. I wondered how she felt about her mother and the grandmother who was so important to her. I wished I'd asked more details about her violin playing, her career, about aging, about facing death.

One afternoon, walking in the vineyard and thinking of the questions I wished I'd asked, an astonishing thought arose. I had spent many years complaining that my mother wanted me to conform to her image of a good daughter instead of trying to see me as a unique individual. I pitied myself that I had been stuck with such a demanding, controlling mother. Now, years after her death, standing in the middle of a block of Pinot Noir vines, I suddenly saw a different scenario. All the while I was criticizing my mother for not valuing me as an individual, I was doing the same thing to her. I had an image in my mind of the mother I wanted her to be, one she never measured up to. I had never tried to know her as the singular individual she was. It was a humbling realization, one that brought to mind the old Pogo cartoon: "We have met the enemy and he is us."

After that thought, which struck like a thunderbolt, an odd thing happened. When I stopped focusing on my mother's inadequacies, I started thinking about her in a new way. She became my Mama. The more arms-length title of Mother fell away. Happy childhood memories, suppressed for years, flooded in: putting on my best dress, patent leather shoes and little white gloves to go with Mama to the ballet; taking the train to Chicago to visit the Museum of Science and Industry and shop at the original Marshall Field's Department Store; starting early in December to bake and decorate fancy Christmas cookies, wrap them in waxed paper and store them in red and green Christmas tins for when my brothers would come home; playing dress up and tea party with me and my dolls.

I thought of the small blue trunk that opened to a wardrobe of doll clothes she had made for me while I was near death with a ruptured appendix just before my fifth birthday. I remember having a terrible stomach ache and being rushed to the hospital. The doctor gave me a fifty percent chance of survival. Mama often told me how anxious she was, how she passed the time sewing doll clothes for me, and how Penicillin, a new drug, saved me. As a child, every time she'd mention the operation, a wave of guilt swept over me. I thought she was trying to make me feel bad about putting her through such an awful time. Suddenly I saw the love and understood what she must have gone through.

All the handcrafts Mama learned from her mother and grandmother, she taught me – embroidery, crochet, needlepoint, knitting. I learned to knit during the Korean War, when her church circle was knitting squares for blankets for the troops. She started me on one too so I could participate. My seven year old fingers clumsily pulled the yarn around one needle and over the other. Each stitch was a victory. I measured at the end of each row to see how close I was to completing my square.

One year, her church circle had their holiday bazaar at our house. It was her excuse to decorate. Large evergreen wreaths with bright red ribbons on the front door; pine greens tied with red bows across the fireplace mantle; a large fresh tree with colored lights and shimmery ornaments; red and green candles everywhere. Fragrant smells of Christmas cookies mingled with fresh pine.

The day of the bazaar, women in stylish wool suits and little hats filled the front hall, the dining room, and the living room. I spent most of my time in the dining room, staring endlessly at the bride doll on display, with her blonde hair, fancy white handmade dress and lacy veil. My yearning was not lost on the church ladies. At the end of the bazaar, the doll hadn't sold, and they decided to give it to me. This magical moment popped into my head after many, many years.

It was time to reframe my past, balance my perspective, and see if, even at this late date, I could understand Mama better. I had a few clues about her musical upbringing, which had been a big part of her childhood, including her father's first question when he came home: "Has Phyllis practiced her violin today?" But I didn't know how she chose the violin, how old she was when she started playing, or what kept her going.

I found I could check her college records online, through the University of Illinois student archives. An astounding 149 references to her appeared in the school paper. Some were articles she had written, covering cultural events on campus, but most were about her musical performances. She had been in demand, playing her violin, solo or with others. The references to her indicated that during all four years of college, from 1923 through 1926, she performed at a multitude of college and community functions. During the last year of her life, her reminiscences always returned to her college years and what fun she had. I had discovered why. She had been a star.

Among her things that surfaced after her death was a notebook she started when she was ninety, entitled "Violin Repertoire." Inside, in her delicate, curvy script, she had listed the pieces she performed. The notebook was probably triggered by her going through her stacks of sheet music prior to donating them. What a list it was: Chopin's Nocturnes, Brahms' Hungarian Dances, works by Schubert, Sarasate, Kreisler, Elgar, Lalo, Bruch, Mozart, Bach, Beethoven. A little note at the end of nine pages said, "110 individual solos."

My oldest brothers remember hearing Mama play her violin in quartets at home when they were little. I don't remember seeing her play, but I do recall listening to a small homemade recording Daddy made. She was playing the Hora Staccato, which she always referred to as "my old warhorse." In the middle of her performance, Daddy, who was holding the microphone, sneezed. My brothers and I liked to listen for the sneeze, which for us was the high point of the recording. I knew she had been first violin in the Chicago Women's Symphony, but what struck me about that was not her prowess, but that women were not allowed to play with men in the big symphony and had to form their own. I grew up loving violin music and associating the violin with my mother, but I never saw her play.

After college she had formed a professional group using a stage name, "Phyllis Farel and her All Girls Band," which travelled throughout the Midwest, then New York City, playing at events ranging from auto shows to trotting races. Girl bands were trendy in the late 1920s and early 30s. She never talked to me about the other "girls" in her group or what it was like having a girl's band. Now I wished I knew more. A 1928 publicity photo of her and her band is all that remains. I can only look at these stylish young women in their flapper dresses and marcelled hair, posed next to their instruments, and imagine what their lives were like. Single, attractive, talented, traveling, and earning good money made for a glamorous life for young women in the 1920s. Wrapped up in my own world, I never asked her the questions I now wanted answers to.

Mama gave up her violin career in 1930 when she married and became pregnant. She was twenty-five, practically a spinster, before she married. Her own mother had been married at eighteen to Leon Feingold, a young physician identified as marriage material by Mama's Grandma Richter. Dr. Feingold had visited their house on a sick call. When Grandma Richter learned he was single, Mama told me, her father never had a chance.

I never knew any of my grandparents since they had all died by the time I was born. I begged Mama to tell me stories about when she was little, always especially drawn to her Grandma Richter who seemed so central to Mama's childhood. Grandma Richter, who emigrated from Russia with her husband and young family when she was twenty-six, seems to have been the template for my mother – a charismatic matriarch who dominated the extended family.

Like my mother, she was forward-thinking in some ways and conservative in others. When a singing teacher told Grandma Richter that her daughter, Rosalia (Mama's mother), had such a beautiful singing voice, she should have it trained, Grandma Richter replied her daughter could use it singing her babies to sleep. On the other hand, when her husband followed his old world custom of putting a sugar lump in his mouth and drinking his tea through it, she chided him that they were in a new country and needed to leave the old ways; he should follow the American custom of putting the sugar in the teacup and stirring it.

Mama regaled me with such vignettes. A talented seamstress, Grandma Richter sewed clothes for my mother, copying them from the latest fashions in the department stores. For a treat, she carved an orange, making a little basket with a handle out of the rind, then filled it with fruit. I loved hearing stories about how her mother and grandma would bake for the holidays, stretching strudel dough across the kitchen table until they could read the newspaper through it.

I feel an energetic through line to the great grandmother I never knew, a strong, creative woman whose only outlet for expressing her power was through her children and her home. My mother found herself in the same position when she gave up her musical career. My brothers and I suffered her displaced power. I grew up sensing frustration, suppressed and unacknowledged, while Mama searched for something to interest her and fill the time. The vineyard and winery gave me another channel, relieving my children of the burden of being the only venue for the controlling energy that seems to be my heritage.

My brother Ronnie looked at me when I met him in London five years after mother's death. It was the first time I'd seen him since then. "Do you know how much you look like Mother?" he asked. This wasn't news. Since I was little Mama's friends had patted my head and told me I was her "spitting image." It never failed to annoy me. "Am not!" I'd say to myself. But the older I get, the more I feel the bond.

I see my mother staring back when I look in the mirror. My deep set eyes are her eyes. I have the same lines around my mouth. She is in me, and this both unnerves and strangely comforts me. I am fascinated by how connected I feel to her – a feeling I fought while she was alive but which now I treasure. So, when Ronnie mentioned it, I recognized the connection. "I always have," I admitted, adding "she was so much more glamorous."

"She lived in a more glamorous age," he replied gently. He was right. Mother came of age in the "Roaring '20s." I thought of her fashion conscious clothes, carefully dyed and coiffed hair, flawless makeup, and brightly polished nails. I came of age in the 1960s, an age known for mismatched prints, jeans, and tie-dye. The closest I came to glamour were the years of my presidency when I dyed my hair blonde. When I want a good laugh, I look at pictures from my blonde phase.

Mama and I looked at the world through the eyes of our times, bookends of the 20th century, both times of explosive change. When my mother was born, in 1905, the car and telephone were novelties, air travel nonexistent. Women couldn't vote and had little legal standing. The worlds we grew up in were miles apart. No wonder when we tried to communicate, our words went askew, heard and interpreted through our generational bias.

Alison and I showed the perspectives of our two generations as we each spoke to the assembled group. As my part of our keynote, I wanted to convey to the current membership the story of how Women for WineSense (WWS) started and the important role it had played in the 1990s, a critical time as the American wine industry expanded. I spoke about its founding in 1990, a time when anti-alcohol forces were gaining momentum and had lumped wine into the catch-all category of "drugs and alcohol."

I had seen prohibition forces at work when Alison started the DARE (Drug Abuse Resistance Education) program, a scare approach aimed at grade school students. She came home horrified that her parents imbibed alcohol. We had to convince her that her parents weren't villains because they made wine. Bill and I had encouraged our kids to take a sip of our wine at dinner and try to describe what they tasted, but after taking the class, Alison refused to let her lips even touch the glass, afraid she would become addicted. I had grown up understanding wine as part of a family meal and wanted our children to do the same.

Women for WineSense was the antidote to the prohibition forces, stating that wine in moderation was part of a healthy, balanced lifestyle; that most wineries were family farms; that wine was part of a good meal. That was our view at Sokol Blosser too. We were thrilled when, in the early 1990s, wine and health were married in the "French Paradox." Scientific proof that red wine bolstered heart health probably did more than anything to disentangle wine from the "drugs and alcohol" category and give it the special place it now holds. Dr. Curtis Ellison, Chief of the Department of Preventive Medicine and Epidemiology at the Boston University School of Medicine and one of the researchers for the French Paradox study, helped give wine its unique niche when he proclaimed: "A glass of wine each day could be more effective at preventing heart attacks than lowering your cholesterol."

After I spoke, Alison took over the microphone to give her perspective on growing up in the wine business. This was the first time I had seen her talk before a group since she introduced me in Toronto in 2007, six years earlier. She stood to take the microphone, her protruding belly prominent through her fitted outfit, her demeanor poised and confident. None of her fatigue or preoccupation with issues back at the office showed. An inveterate teacher, my comments had been a historic look at the wine industry, serious and educational. Alison's became a cheerful counterpoint.

I looked at her in wonder as I found myself laughing along with the rest of the women. This poised, funny person was the same timid young woman who overcame timidity to stand in for me at a winery dinner in Toronto six years before. Alison had the audience's enthusiastic attention as she described growing up in a family so business-oriented that their idea of vacation was working a wine festival, not playing at Disneyland. She talked about what made her want to come back to the family business. "When I went to college," she said, "I became determined to work in the real world. I wanted a real job so I could make real money." She stopped here and looked around. With a dramatic pause, she added her confession, "Well, folks, I learned the real world is not all it's cracked up to be. It didn't take long for me to realize that working for my family in our family business was a dream job."

She explained how we spent three years transitioning from me, a single president, to her and her brother as co-presidents. "The co-presidency is a unique model and one everyone told us was fraught with challenges," she said. "However, as you may have figured out by now, my family never takes the easy route." Someone asked what it was like working with her brother. "It's honestly great fun," she said. "Yes, there are times I want to strangle him. And," she added, continuing her sisterly frankness, "we're very different people. But we have a deep love and loyalty not just to each other but also to our shared vision and common goal to be amazing stewards of our business so that we can hand it off to the next generation in even better shape and with even more opportunities than we received it." I tried not to puff up like the proverbial Jewish mother, but I had an urge to gesture and exclaim, "My daughter the President!"

Alison left the gathering right after dinner. I walked her part way to her car, wishing I could smooth away the worry lines on her face.

"I couldn't believe how funny you were tonight," I told her. "Especially since I know how worn out you are." Alison stopped and looked at me.

"Mom," she said. "I'm a serious person. That was the professional me talking. I was acting." Then she grinned. "I learned it from you," she finished. I could only smile. "I love you, babe," I said, as I gave her a hug. "I love you too, Mom," and she opened the door to get in her car.

Epilogue

When I began to tell my story, I thought I was writing a business book, an account of the transition from first to second generation in my family business. My story would function as a case study of the challenges, a way to help other family business owners who had kids involved, or really anyone who faced letting go of something meaningful to them. Sharing what I went through would show that, despite the pain, it was possible to move on to something equally satisfying. A friend had told me: "When one door closes, another opens. But it's hell in the hallway." My story would demonstrate that truth. As I spelled out the difficulty I'd had surrendering control and creating my future, writing became a process of discovery. Like the ribbon ball gifts popular in my childhood, unwinding liberated a succession of surprises. Ribbon balls yielded trinkets or charms; what I unwound were tensions, conflicts, and assumptions that had wallpapered my inside.

I started with the question I kept asking all through the transition: why was giving up control so difficult for me? I had initiated the process and wanted to do it. Why was it so traumatic? This led me back to my childhood to start unraveling my ribbon ball of life. One trinket that fell out was a glimpse into the divided self I had learned to live with. Who was the real me? Was I the self-assured, assertive persona I presented, or the unsure, subservient personality I often felt myself to be? That split got more convoluted. Underneath my confident persona lurked self-doubt. Below my submissive mode lay fierce independence. I had lived with this disharmony for so long that clenching my teeth to keep going felt normal. The more I wrote, the deeper I went inside.

Seen from the outside, the switch from first generation to second appeared uneventful – a textbook case of family business transition. People complimented us on our seamless accomplishment. Oregon State University's prestigious Family Business Program awarded me and Sokol Blosser Winery the Director's Award for exemplary family business practices, based on the smoothness of our transition. Five of us went on stage to accept. Nik brought his eleven year old son, Alexander (named for his Uncle Alex), to represent the third generation. He looked out from the stage with wonder at the full ballroom of guests applauding us.

Behind the honorary plaque lay the understory of my emotional turbulence, trying to swap out my skill at accumulating, and learn instead the art of letting go. That involved moving from a platform of scarcity and competition to one of abundance and contribution. Without a doubt, the winery transition was the biggest challenge and toughest work of my thirty years of business. Turning control of the business into the hands of my children, I had no reservations about their ability – they were capable, energetic, and creative. It was all about my letting go.

We face letting go repeatedly throughout our lives. A governor leaving office gives up being the center of attention, a staff at the ready, a driver and state police escort, as he or she returns to being an ordinary citizen. But the emotional challenge of letting go on that scale is no different from what a mother feels sending her last child off to college. Because we emphasize getting there – campaigning for governor and preparing for school – we don't talk much about the aftermath.

Usually seen as the end, letting go also gives us opportunity for a beginning. My business transition opened a gateway that triggered continued personal transformation, letting go in multiple ways. I can only smile at my naiveté when I think of how straightforward and uncomplicated the process seemed when I first embarked on it. If I'd known how lengthy and emotionally charged it would be, would I have still done it? Absolutely. But I'm glad I didn't know.

Despite my difficulty in letting go of the winery, there is a simplicity to it compared to the complex layers of family bonds. Painful as it was, it was essentially a one time event, whereas letting go in the context of family means ongoing modifications. Raising children requires a continuing process of letting go. As parents, we start with total control and learn to let go (or not) with each growth spurt. As children mature and our lives change, we constantly redefine our roles. I will always be mother to my children, but we will interact differently as we age. I have had to learn to deal with Alex and Alison in diverse roles. My primary role has switched from boss to Mom. My motherly concerns for their welfare take priority. They became my boss when my Founder title continued my winery employ. As part of the winery's board of directors, I govern their employment. Sometimes I need to identify, for myself as well as for them, which hat I'm wearing.

My estrangement from Alex ended four years after he became co-president. Our relationship revived when he invited me to accompany him on a European trip. I knew Alex was planning to travel to London for the winery. I suggested we fly over together when my brother, Ronnie, whom I hadn't seen since mother's death, invited me to meet him in London where all his sons were living. Alex said we could travel to London, his first stop, together, but that he would be going on from there. Then, several weeks later, casually, like there had been no rift in our relationship, he said, "Mom, one of our barrel suppliers has invited me to visit. He's in the Champagne area. Do you want to come with me? We could spend the week in London, the weekend in France, and then fly to Stockholm." I tried to keep the excitement out of my voice. Just as casually, I said, "Alex, I've wanted to visit the French oak forests since I started running the winery. Visiting a stave mill would be great, and I'd love to see Stockholm." Letting him go had brought us back together.

Seeing how well Alex and Alison had moved into their presidential roles made me reflect on how much the family board of Sokol Blosser Winery had also evolved since I surrendered control. No longer my rubber stamp, the board had become a team, needing every member's attention and expertise. When Alex and Alison took over, knowing their inexperience, we took pains to meet more often, demand constant reporting, and generally keep the young pups on a tight leash. Bill and Nik stepped up as I took a back seat.

Bill accompanied Alison on a European trip, represented the winery at wine dinners, and poured at tastings around the country. At board meetings, his planning background and experience running a corporate office helped him ask the right questions. Nik, although working overtime to build his own business and spend time with his young family, took on the role of chair with great seriousness, pressuring the co-presidents for additional information necessary to make informed decisions, combing financial projections for possible problems, questioning plans for achieving sales goals, and generally bringing his judicious and strategic mind to bear on winery policy. Through a combination of cheerleading support and keen oversight, the five of us grew closer. I watched Alex and Alison learn to work together, both supporting and questioning each other.

A feature distinctive to a family business, or maybe just peculiar to our family, was open acknowledgement of each of our individual weaknesses as well as our strengths. We are blunt, confronting each other as only family members could do.

"Mom, you're the Great Triangulator, but you've got to let them figure it out for themselves," Alex told me when he saw me trying to fix a disagreement. He was right and I appreciated his reining me in. Knowing that love underlies our interactions has made unnecessary the finesse one would use with employees.

When family ties renewed, the five of us, Bill and I and our three kids, started getting together again as a family, for holidays, trips and BBQs, including our new spouses. Each of us, except Nik, had new partners. The winery, which in some sense had split us up, had brought us together again.

Our roles had changed and we looked different. Now silver-haired, the images of Bill in his French beret planting vines and me in braids driving the tractor existed only in our memories and old photos. The two of us had taken on the support roles our parents had played. Our kids were driving the bus. Their children, Bill's and my grandchildren, the third generation of Sokol Blosser Winery, were in driver training. We were a family business. My Daddy would be so proud.

Telling my story also showed how much I was a product of my era. My path followed the feminist tenor of the times. My generation not only challenged conventional male-female relationships, but reshaped them along the way. Born in the 1940s and liberated by the birth control revolution of the late 20th century, we fought for equal rights for women in every arena, from public school athletics to workplace equality. We started from the Victorian stance of our mothers, then changed the playing field when we came of age in the last third of the 20th century, courted, married, and raised families. At every stage, I belonged to a circle of women who shared stories and advice. I never had a mentor, but I had friends in the same boat. With no blueprint, only our ideals, to guide us, we tried to balance career and children, love and independence, heredity and innovation, determined to go where women had not gone before.

When I went to Stanford University in 1962 as a freshman, the university took parental responsibility for their coeds. Women students had curfews of 10:00 PM on weekdays and midnight on Saturdays. We had to sign out, telling where we were going, with whom, and what time we returned. Denouncing in loco parentis became a rallying cry. By the time I graduated four years later, women's social regulations had almost disappeared. I spent my senior year in the university's first student resident high rise apartment, able to come and go as I pleased, unthinkable four years earlier. The position of Dean of Women had disappeared as Dean of (all) Students took over.

Reshaping gender roles continues, but a new challenge has been added – redefining old age. My generation has entered "la troisieme," the last third of life, and the aging process has my full attention. I'm watching myself grow old, a spectator, as well as a participant. Still physically fit and mentally active, traditional retirement has no relevance. We've broken the mold, but have no replacement. I want to grow old gracefully, but I'm not sure what that means. As my friends and I seek to be worthy elders, we find ourselves forging a new model of aging. Our success with gender relations gives us courage. We are used to making it up as we go.

In my mind, aging falls in the category of experiences one has to live through to understand – experiences that can be appreciated but not fully grasped by study, or even observation. After I had my first child, I decided giving birth fell in that category. None of the numerous books or birthing classes prepared me for the actual experience. Giving birth graphically established what I had only known intellectually – that the body parts I associated with sexual arousal had utilitarian functions. I wasn't used to thinking of my uterus, vagina, and breasts as a complex miracle of sequential engineering. Having to experience giving birth excludes one gender, but aging is gender neutral, open to all who survive.

Seeing the years pass with increasing speed, watching one's parents and friends, young and old, die off, with no regard to their goodness or importance, drives home the reality of how fleeting we are, how fragile life is. It's hard to remember how inviolate we felt in our youth. My kids listen and nod when I try to explain the physical and mental changes I've experienced, but I know old age seems far away and irrelevant. It certainly did to me as I watched my parents.

Aging has been full of surprises. While the physical may be in decline, the mental and emotional have grown stronger. I am amazed to find more joy in my life than ever. Power and success – happiness as our world defines it – can be won by fighting hard enough. It's the triumph of one's outer self. But joy, peace, and love come from inside. I had to become an elder to claim that. An inverse relationship between body and brain has come with aging. No longer fresh-faced and agile, the wrinkling of my body parallels the strengthening of my mind. My bodysuit may be less attractive, but I feel more comfortable in it.

What I sensed at my sixtieth birthday was that it was time for me to stop working towards power and prestige. I had proved I could attain those. Now was the time to think about stepping back, to find a new passion (although I had no idea then what that might be) and to start giving away the knowledge I had gained from my experience. Then, it was a tiny thought with no idea how to do it. I hadn't seen any guide books explaining how to pass the mantle responsibly and lovingly. But I recognized it as my next step. The curtain I had passed through put me on the performance stage of letting go. And in letting go, I discovered life beyond: beyond what I had done my whole adult life, beyond retirement, beyond youth. Lao Tzu's quote "When I let go of what I am, I become what I might be," says it all. Clearly, I'm not the first person to make this discovery. Lao Tzu lived in the 6th century BC. His quote also points to a corollary to letting go – becoming.

This book is my story of becoming, of bringing the pieces of myself, divided since childhood, into alignment. Letting go of the public persona that had dominated my life turned into a story of integrating the parts of me that had been suppressed for so many years. I was trying to do what the most sophisticated scientists have done – pull the physical and metaphysical together. Albert Einstein denounced their artificial separation: "The intuitive mind is a sacred gift and the rational mind is a faithful servant. We have created a society that honors the servant and has forgotten the gift."

Our lives bear an up and down rhythm of good and difficult times. Neither last. We yearn for stability but there is no such thing. As a child, I envisioned being grown up as a fixed state one achieved at a certain age, somewhere really old, like thirty. Adults reinforced this idea by always asking: "What do you want to be when you grow up?" I learned to have an answer ready, although I've never been any of the professions I imagined between ages five and twenty – jockey, ballerina, United Nations translator, attorney, historian. Instead I've done things I'd never imagined – farmer, business owner, author, political candidate, nonprofit founder.

When I presided over Sokol Blosser, my life had predictability. Going to the winery every day, I could forecast, within certain limits, what I would be doing in the years ahead. When I look at what I've done since leaving the winery, what stands out is how unpredictable going forward has been. Even as close as six months from inception, I would never have predicted I would embark on a spiritual journey, run for political office, or start a nonprofit organization. Retirement was simply a stop for redirection.

"What will you do," is the wrong question, anyway. "Who are you," is the right one. It's not about what I'm going to do as much as it's about the kind of person I will be doing it. Whatever I choose to do, my inner and outer layers will be aligned. Well-being comes when they work together. Buddhists articulate this as the union of wisdom and compassion, a fusion appropriate whether running a business, entering politics, or playing with grandchildren.

Out in the vineyard, a pair of red tailed hawks ride the wind currents high above the vines. A redwing blackbird whistles its mournful cry from a nearby pond. Bluebirds and finches flutter in the vine canopy, poking for insects, while swallows swoop and swirl to catch them in the air. The soil quivers with its web of small creature activity. Trails of pushed up earth between telltale mounds reveal subterranean activity as moles and gophers till the soil in their search for food. From high in the sky to deep underground, the earth hums with life – all part of this complex, inextricably interdependent wonder. Life, boisterous, diverse, and fragile, carries on.

Index